I0235880

GOD'S AUDACITY:
The Logic of GOD'S EXISTENCE

Books by Samuel K. Anderson

1. God's Audacity: The Logic of God's Existence.

2. Whispers from My Mother.

3. Human's Audacity: The Leadership in Everyone.

4. The Kind Prince and Princess (Children's Book edition)

GOD'S AUDACITY:
The Logic of GOD'S EXISTENCE

An Epistemological, Mathematical, Biblical, Geographical, Archaeological, Scientific, Common Sense and Cultural Approach to Searching and Intellectually Embracing the Logic of God's Existence.

by

Samuel K. Anderson

Royal Publication

New Jersey, U.S.A

God's Audacity: The Logic of God's Existence.

Copyright © 2019 Samuel K. Anderson.

All rights reserved. No part of this book may be reproduced or used in any manner without written permission of the copyright owner except for the use of quotations in a book review.

Published November 2019

ISBN-10: 1-7340066-0-9

ISBN-13: 978-1-7340066-0-5 (Trade Hardback)

Royal Publication

434 Kearny Ave. #200

Kearny, New Jersey 07032

royalpublication@aol.com

God's Audacity: The Logic of God's Existence.

This book is fervently dedicated to my children:

Serenity and Samuel 2nd

TABLE OF CONTENTS

CHAPTER 1

CHAPTER 1

INTRODUCTION

GOD'S AUDACITY: The Logic of GOD'S EXISTENCE

The logic of God's existence is a logic of wisdom in

pursuit of God's *reality, Omnipotence, Omnipresence,*

Supremeness of Love Epitomized, Omniscient, Holiness,

Eternally Unchanging, The Great I AM, The God of

Everything, God is God, and everything known and

unknown to the brittle mortal mind of humanity. I would

like to humbly emphasize that it is unquestionably grueling

to define *The One True Omnipotent God*. This book is

seeking, knocking and questing to logically and educatively

rationalize this logic of intuition through the lens of

mathematical formula, scientific, archaeological, biblical,

1

geological, cultural, and the philosophy of common-sense approach to analyzing God's existence and his being. Do not forget that this is a spiritual journey too. Every history, culture, or language known and unknown to mankind under the sun, above the sun or beneath the planets has an idea about *The Most High God.* No matter how hard one may attempt to fight it or pretend to deny such intelligent magnitude of existence; the fact remains irrefutable.

The most complex mission for any human to embark on is the one relating to the topic of *The One True God.* Interestingly, regardless of one's religion, faith, association, movement or identification; whenever the topic or subject of *The Most High* comes up, we all seem to be interested to find the answers. That "curiosity" indicates the hidden facet of a yearning desire to find our way back to our true source. The *unmatched force of omnipotent energy,* that which is bigger, greater and infinite to our human mind is our source. The faint voice of our curiosity which resides dominantly within our pineal gland, that which was created to flow through our medulla oblongata is hungry to reconnect with its source of being. Among other questions this book would answer constitutes: How is God (*The One True Omnipotent God)* the source of everything? What is consciousness? What are the levels of spirituality? Is there any archaeological finding to support what we have read about *The One True Omnipotent God's* existence? How does mankind relate to *The Most High God*? What's the nature, character and attributes of *The One True Omnipotent God.* How does mankind's activity, culture, and actions directly or indirectly reflect the existence of *The One True Omnipotent God?* Why should I even care about *The Most High's* existence or inexistence? Who are the *Annunaki* or *Fallen Angels*? Can mathematics and science support *The Most High's* existence? The philosophy of common sense has been pushed throughout this writing for us to use, should we ever need it. In a candid logic of reasoning, the philosophy of common sense

and wisdom is far greater than knowledge. In that,

knowledge can be manipulated and controlled but wisdom

always reign supreme. You are also encouraged in this

book to use any available ethical means to research about

what you are reading or studying in this book. I highly

encourage you to not expect to be spoon fed throughout this

book. I made some references in this book that may require

you to research. I believe this would help us to learn more

and acquire great deal of information for our personal

relationships (solely at our discretion) with *The One True*

Omnipotent God.

Our current world is filled with impressive

intellectuals, theories, concepts, ethical leaders and free

thinkers. There are also lot of religious groups, beliefs,

pessimists, optimists, and non-believers. We all have the

freedom to make and take decisions daily a.k.a *Free Will.*

Hence, you have the freedom to believe in *a god, a thing,*

an object, an entity, nothing at all or The Most High God.

The choice is our individual mandate to make. Believe it or

not, you have made that choice consciously or

unconsciously as you read this paragraph. Another

interesting part is that (in my humble comprehension),

there is one choice that gives complete peace of mind to the

soul, body and spirit of an individual. That is the choice to

consciously and spiritually embrace *The One True*

Omnipotent Creator. It comes with great difficulty to solely

use our mortal concept of worldly acquired knowledge to

attempt to fully comprehend the spiritual brobdingnagian

power of *The One True Omnipotent God.* We need to

consciously and spiritually transform within ourselves into

higher levels of ourselves capable and willing to unlearn

everything and to relearn that which is not visible to the

naked eye. If you feel that self-reliance through acquired

knowledge in a specific field of study is enough to decide

on the validity of *The Most High God* (which needs no

validation by the way); then you will be stupefied when it comes to *The Most High Creator* and the stupendous creations in the universe.

To the impious, sacrilegious and nullifidian; I say to you, read this book with fresh perspective to be able to have fair introspection. To the science fanatics, archaeologists, astronomers, mathematicians, philosophers, darwinism, the big-bang believers or followers and various fields of studies; it's a pleasure to have you on board to read and study this book. I acknowledge and appreciate the knowledge acquired in various fields of study. I strongly believe in a logical inclination that we are all playing at *The Most High's* backyard with all the research, digging, mining in space and on land trying to see the magnificence in and around the universe. To the apostate, welcome aboard; fasten your seat belt for a ride through the old awareness and the new awareness. To the agnostics and every type of skeptics out there, this book covers your concern too. I am seriously writing this very line with a smile on my face, welcome aboard everyone and enjoy this ride. To all atheist far and near, your disbelief in *The Most High's* existence is well noted. I hope the epistemological, scientific and logical study covered in this book will motivate you to enjoy reading this book. Finally, to the pious, theists, Christians, Catholics, every religious denominations or groups and the rest of mankind; I hope you all read this book with a humble heart, open mentality with no dogmatism and any other *isms*. This book is not a religious book, because *The Most High* doesn't ascribe to a religion (which is man-made). It is a book for all humanity. To anyone willing and desiring to learn more about *The One True Omnipotent God.* I wrote this book with an open heart and mind to welcome every human being regardless of the belief, faith, gender, nationality or origination. If you read this book with a closed mind, you will miss almost everything in it. You will need to use reason to understand, logic to aid you to see consistency and be objective to use reality to gain some relations with this book. You ought to be rational.

Final words, the most powerful weapon effective to destabilize the strength, power, intellectual agility, and the union of any friendship, relationship, family, community, institutions, municipality, a state/region or a nation is the seed of discord. Once effectively sowed, you can easily control, manipulate and destroy such people's identity, confidence, knowledge and their very worth. Such distorted people will believe anything outside of themselves. This book (*God's Audacity: The Logic of God's Existence*) will challenge you to question everything, be rational, aid you to understand science, philosophy, sociology, physics, technology, mathematics, cultures, archaeology, the philosophy of common sense and your very own spirituality of consciousness.

It is more than just a read; it is a study. So, I hope you are ready for a hiking journey. Some of us may need to read and study it a couple of times before grasping the core of this journey. Are you ready to explore?

CHAPTER 2

CHAPTER 2

THE MATHEMATICAL EQUATION/FORMULA OF GOD'S EXISTENCE

Mathematics is directly connected to physics and engineering. Mathematics is literally in everything we do in life, even the simplest things. We all use numbers, quantities of entities and space in our daily lives. Etymologically and epistemologically, mathematics is as vital as every field of study. In a logical approach, mathematics is in every known culture of mankind. This unfolds the basic commonality linking mankind to a powerful way to communicate, calculate and comprehend the world we live in and the universe out there in general. It is not uncommon to see mathematical statements in the *Bible, Quran*, every religious books and cultures.

Hence, the relevance of mathematics to logically discuss God's existence cannot be stressed enough. You will however need to always apply humility through the usage of the philosophy of common sense when it comes to the study or discussion of God's existence. In that, everything we are seeing now and the things yet to come have already existed in the past. There is nothing new under the sun, if anything; we are only trying to catch up. It's my encouragement that this awareness will put you into the realm of deep thinking to gain a revelation of *The Most High's* greatness. As the dicopomorpha echmepterygis a.k.a the Fairyfly is nothing but the tiniest insect on our planet comparable to the size of humans so are humans like dicopomorpha echmepterygis (with direct respect to size) in the realm of *The Most High Creator*.

Characteristically, your mind is the most powerful key to unlock the attributes of *The Most High*. The philosophy of common sense in this situation is simply pure wealth. Knowledge then becomes one of life's many blessings. Wisdom *is* and *will* always be supreme as well as the epitome of *The Most High's* simplest dimple of grace, essence, presence and nature. *The logic of God's existence formula or equation* is a mathematical educative approach to use the knowledge procured through formal or informal education to comprehend *The Most High God* and the things created by *Him*. You are encouraged to use this lore in mathematics to follow through what I am about to logically unfold.

The Logic of God's Existence Formula/Equation.

$$X = \infty$$
$$X + 1 = \infty$$
$$X = \infty - 1$$
$$X = X$$

Variable denotations:

X = denotes God (*The One and Only True Almighty God*), The Great I AM, Omnipotence, Omnipresence, Omniscient, Holiest Holiness, Eternal Super Hypernova Radiant Preeminent Energy, Spirit of all spirits, Light of all lights, Force of all forces, The Source of Everything known and unknown to every creation.

X=X => denotes, God is God. There is none before God and none after God. *The Most High God* is Everything.

∞ = denotes the Infinite Universe, Space, Vacuum, Nothingness Realm, Realms unknown to mankind and every living creation, Space in Time and Dimensional realms measurable and immeasurable, God's Canvas for all His creative work. The infinite space within which everything and nothing exists both living and non-living to the naked eye, rays, beams, lasers, or sounds.

16

Logically, ∞ then contains everything "**1**" represents since

∞ is *The Most High God*, the Creator's canvas for all *His*

awe-inspiring works.

1 = denotes Angels, You, I, Mankind, Trees, Oceans,

Atmosphere, Rocks, Minerals, Life, Death, Good, Evil,

Languages, everything that exists in and around the

universe and realms known and unknown to mankind and

all creatures in material, immaterial and spiritual realms.

Further Explanation of the Logic of God's Existence mathematical formula/equation

A) X + 1

God and *His* imagined creativity before *He* spoke it into

reality. **1** came out of **X**, with **1** representing everything

God created. We should be open to learn that God

"*thought*" about everything *He* was about to create and

knew very well how to create them. **X + 1** is the inspiration

of *God* just like an artist gets an inspiration before creating

that specific art in a creative manifestation to the world.

B) $\infty - 1$

The canvas of **X**, what *The Most High* created **1** from; that

is out of ∞ (nothing, Space, Vacuum). Humans are part of **1**

and with humans, our flesh was formed from the soil (after

X created the earth which contain the soil out of ∞).

C) X = ∞

X *is* and *has* been everything and **X** is infinite in the sense

of eternity. **X** existed even when there was nothing, empty

Space, Vacuum, and no time; **X** is preeminent and the

Ancient of Days. In the existence of **X** exists ∞.

D) "1" can never be ---→ 1= ∞ - X

This is the abomination Lucifer (who later was cursed by **X**

and became satan, the devil) committed. The laughable

attempt to rule over **X** and become **X** in **X's** own realm.

Some humans, who are also a representation of **1**

consciously and unconsciously try to become a *"god"*;

asked other humans to worship, praise, serve, call and see

them as a *"god"*. Even some humans in religious roles, kingdoms, and other earthly high offices demand to be granted the title of a *god*; in hopes and quests to become **X**. This is the sin of pride **"1"** continuously commits and complete chaos comes with it (fall of mankind).

Since **X's** nature constitutes *Free Will*, *He* granted it to humans (a representation within **1**). The *Free Will* sets humans apart to *freely* choose to fulfil the *Will* of **X** *(The Most High God)*. The *Creator* will not allow disorder, chaos, blasphemy and anything contrary to **X's** *being* and *Will* to continue. Mankind's acts to become a *god* will never happen because the *creation* can never rule over *The Creator*. What you just read above is summarized in a mathematical language below:

a) $\mathbf{X} + \mathbf{1}$ b) $\infty - \mathbf{1}$

c) $\mathbf{X} = \infty$ d) $\mathbf{1} \# \infty - \mathbf{X}$ (1 is not equal to $\infty - X$)

Diagrammatically and Figuratively.

Diagrammatically, let's have a look at *figure 1* below as a further emphasis on this mathematical logic of representation to help those of us who are more visual. Also, *fig.5* under *chapter 4* should be referenced for a higher level of understanding and explanation.

Fig.1

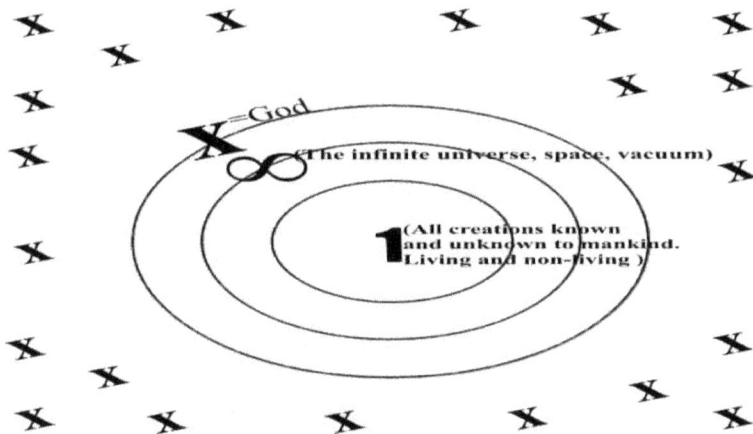

1 is within ∞ as ∞ is within **X**. Alternatively, **X** contains ∞ and within ∞ exists 1; meaning everything both existing to the knowledge of mankind and the ones unknown to us fall within God's (**X's**) realms and being.

X through ∞ to **1** has provided what is called *Free Will* to a specific group of creation within **1** *called* humans even the angels, demons and other spirits do not have the luxury of *Free Will.* Humans (a representation within **1**) have the freedom to think, design, create, reproduce, and the freedom to choose however and whatever decision they desire. The *Free Will* gives mankind the audacity to decide to either consciously connect in worship, communication and fellowship with **X** or consciously disconnect with **X** and to directly worship objects, spirits, materials, entities within ∞. Logically, deciding to worship entities within or through ∞ is a direct disrespect, dishonor, disobedience and disruption of the perfect harmonic flow of energy to **X.** Since **X** is *Omnipotent* and *The Creator* of everything within ∞. **X's** _desire_ has simply been for humans (a representation within **1**) to _directly_ relate, communicate, worship and fellowship in _oneness_ with Him; **X**. The *Free Will* is part of the many special things that make humans special, without it; we may basically be spiritual "robots" in an earthly body. **X's** *core* is ***love*** and it is out of love that everything within **1** was created through ∞. It is humans' *Free Will* to choose that may possess either a negative (-) or positive (+) energy of influence (I will explain this concept into details in *chapter 4*). The current confusion in and around our world is due to the misuse and abuse of **1's** *Free Will*. When **X** created everything out of nothing (∞, His canvas), **X** said; everything consisted in **1** with ∞ was perfect. Hence, **X** as *The Creator*, has the audacity and will use this audacity to realign everything into perfection as intended from *alpha* to *omega* in the formula and equation; $X = \infty$, $X + 1 = \infty$ and $X = \infty - 1$.

As a reinforcement, **X** is the creator of **1**, hence **1** is **X's** creation. *The Creator*, **X** can clean, recreate, or repair all the creations within **1** at any time to **X's** *satisfaction* and *discretion*. With respect to *time*, **X** is outside the realms of ∞; *time* is under the control of **X** and relative to all creations (living and non-living, physical and spiritual) within **1** and ∞. The *time* with which **X** will put everything within ∞ back to order is only known, controlled, and initiated by **X** and **X** alone. Irrespective of **1's** attempts to consciously or unconsciously reject, fight, or deny **X**; **X** *is* and *will* remain **X** at all times.

Rhetorical Logics

Scenario I

Let's have a look at this scenario; use *logic* to follow through:

Y = denotes human creator, builder or inventor.

P = denotes the "Product" created or invented by Y.

C = denotes Consumers or Users.

Y creates or build a **P** to function in a specific way (obviously, in this scenario; whatever **Y** creates, build or invent does not have *Free Will*). **Y** expects **P** to function

according to how it was created, built or invented. **Y** will

put **P** through series of testing, practice, experiments to

make sure the performance of **P** is at par with the expected

function that **P** was created to play/perform. Now, **Y** easily

replicates **P** to have hundreds, thousand, millions or billions

of the product, **P**. When **Y** is fully satisfied with **P**; **Y** then

release, outdoor, or launch **P** to the world of **C**. If **Y** receive

various complains from **C** that **Y's** "**Ps**" are malfunctioning

or not as quality as **Y** proclaimed or advertised. **Y** can

decide to *recall* all malfunctioned **Ps** to *perfect* or *correct*

them since that <u>was</u> and still <u>remain</u> the original grand plan

of **Y** when he/she was creating, building or inventing

his/her **Ps**. **Y** has the *power* to correct malfunctioned **Ps**.

Malfunctioned **Ps** will then go through whatever

"corrected process" or *"engineering"* **Y** has set to

"perfect" the **Ps**. **Y's** *"corrected process"* or

"engineering" for malfunctioned **Ps** could be crushing

them, smashing, mashing, cutting them into pieces or

burning the malfunctioned Ps in a high heat temperature to

be recycled.

Scenario II

Probability in mathematical reasoning is the likelihood of an event or events occurring per the amount/number of possible outcomes.

Hence, **Probability** = $\dfrac{\text{Event (Events)}}{\text{Amount (Number) of Outcomes}}$

I am not going to teach mathematics here. The logic is to aid different minds; in this case those who like math to reason with logic about the existence of *The Most High God, The Creator*. Most importantly, what are your *chances* and *consequences* should you decide to *Freely*, at your own *Free Will*, choose an event of choice that has a **probability of happening** or **not happening**. This is the motive in this scenario.

A] *An Impossible Outcome Probability.*

This is the probability that there is zero chance of an event happening, in that; the outcome is simply zero or better yet undefined, not infinity but undefined. In mathematics, any dividend with which the divisor is zero is simply zero or undefined. Hence, a zero outcome means there is absolutely no chance or probability for an event to happen. This represents *those* who *feel/argue* that there is absolutely _no_ *Most High God, The creator*. This is an insane decision because they (*those who believe in such probable outcome*) have *not* been able to *prove, logically showcase* or *epistemologically researched* to *validate* their stand. In a logical rhetoric, *if* an impossible outcome with respect to the existence of *The Most High God, The creator* (The Most Powerful Energy Undetectable with/by any scientific object) is *plausible*, then life and everything in it has absolute zero essence.

B] *The likelihood of God existing or Not existing. Should you die to find out, what is the probability of God existing?*

The number of outcome(s) = 2

Event = 1

So, this means:

Probability of God Existing = <u>Event</u>

The number of outcome(s)

$$\Rightarrow 1/2 = 0.5 = 50\%$$

The answer for the **Probability of God Existing (in the event of dying to find out)** is 0.5 or 50%. Now, with this mathematical analysis in probability; apply the philosophy of common sense and logic here in analyzing the *possible outcome(s)* with the understanding of *either* believing in *The Most High God's* existence *or not* believing in *The Most High* Creator's existence:

Before we begin, you ought to note that both **Analysis A** and **Analysis B** below are based on an individual _not_ believing in the existence of _The Most High_ Creator.

Analysis A: Should you die and _indeed_ find out that there is **no** _Most High God, The Creator_; then you are obviously free and life just ends, because you are not going to be resurrected back to life after expiring and there is no account to be given, since there is **no** _Most High God._

Analysis B: On the other side of 0.5 or 50%. Should you die and find out that there is _The Most High God, The Creator (The One and Only True Almighty God), Omnipotence, Omnipresence, Omniscient, Holiest Holiness, Eternal Super Hypernova Radiant Preeminent Energy, Spirits of all spirits, Force of all forces, The Source of Everything known and unknown to every creation;_ then you are simply toast, in trouble, or in eternal damnation. In that, life doesn't end after death and you are about to give accounts on how you lived the life that was given to you. How did you perform in exercising your *Free Will* with its accompanied consequences or rewards according to the direction of the <u>*Word*</u> of *The Most High God, Eternal Super Hypernova Radiant Preeminent Energy, Spirits of all spirits, Force of all forces, The One and Only True Almighty God, Omnipotence, Omnipresence, and Omniscient.* This is a mathematical probability you wouldn't want to encounter. All in all, the decision to believe in the existence of *The Most High God* or not to believe lies in your *Free Will.*

Bringing It All Together

We all have *Free Will* married with solid reasoning through the philosophy of common sense and wisdom to *decide* and *choose* what we want or desire to logically believe through faith. I want to slightly go off tangent to talk about *Faith* (I will come back to conclude). Who *controls* and *knows* the probability of waking up tomorrow with *direct respect to human's capabilities*? Exactly, no human knows. There is no scientific formula, mathematical method or physics calculations that can 100% control and know the probability of every human waking up tomorrow or the next day; yet we all plan for tomorrow. We all *believe* to be here by tomorrow, and we all have *faith* that tomorrow would come, and we will be alive. We go through what I will call an *unsure/unguaranteed repetitive probability* of waking up tomorrow and the next day to *hopefully* (another word within the family of *Faith*) retire and enjoy retirement through old age. None of that is guaranteed and yet, we do

31

not have any problem with that *perspective of Faith.*

However, some people struggle *to believe, to have faith* in

the *Existence of The Most High God.*

Back to the tangent of *Free Will*, **X** has given a special

group within His creation, **1** (in this case *Humans* as a

representation within **1**) existing within ∞ the ability to

exercise their *Free Will.* Humans are being handled with

<u>*Grace*</u> granted by **X** on earth. Humans are going to be

handled after we depart from this earthly body *differently*

from all the creations living within ∞. The likes of *all the*

demons, devil, evil spirits, principalities and dark powers

within every realm of ∞ have been already condemned.

They are all going to face the wrath of **X** but *humans* are

yet to be judged to either face **X's** wrath or live with **X**

eternally. **X**, *The Most High, Eternal Super Hypernova*

Radiant Preeminent Energy is *eternal* because, **X** can never

be destroyed **(X = ∞; X = X).** Some of **X's** characteristics

live within **1** which represents all **X's** creations.

32

Additionally, logical reasoning is one of the many gifts in life that costs us nothing to use. The philosophy of *common sense* is one of the most common features within mankind, it is paramount for us to apply this quality in our daily walks to comprehend things about *The Most High*. The art of not believing in **X's** existence with no solid proof of **X's** inexistence is simply the art of unconsciously believing in the probability of **X's** existence. Follow this analogy, if someone doesn't believe in something because he/she does not have the knowledge or understanding of that specific thing's existence that doesn't deny the existence of the entity in question; rather, it exposes the doubter's knowledge deficit and inability to even support with logical reasons to his/her disbelieve in that entity. Consciously or unconsciously, you are a *glimpse* of **X**. The one you seek or struggle to believe through *faith* is already within you. Deducing from the equation/formula discussed in this chapter; "**1**" cannot exist without **X's** existence but

X exists with or without the existence of **1**. **X** exists beyond time, space, realms and all dimensions known and unknown to any living thing both in the physical and spiritual realms within ∞. I want to point out that, one's true freedom is gradually gravitated towards full actualization when one attempts to curiously apply acquired knowledge to wisdom in hopes to comprehend the core basis of the spiritual world and its existence. This freedom is far above the most sophisticated scientific proof of any material and immaterial existence known and unknown to mankind (I hope you can feel my excitement).

Every physical thing made on this physical/material realm is useless in other realms let alone the realm of *The Most High God*. Material things from this material world *(every human invention including houses, cars, planes, technology and even material things created by God such as the human body, animals both on land and in the sea, natural gas, minerals including gold, all the trees, insects et al)* are all going back to the soil with which it came from.

I am talking about both non-biodegradable and

biodegradable things. Mankind's concepts, knowledge and

understanding of this physical realm is just a dust particle

in the sight of the *Omnipotent God*. Anything that is non-

spiritual is perishable. Any *spirit* including that of mankind

that is toxic to the environment of *The Most High* is going

to be recycled in any way *The Most High* deems.

CHAPTER 3

CHAPTER 3

THE "GOD CONSCIOUSNESS" IN EVERYTHING.

Every nation, every language, every dialect, and every race known and unknown to mankind proclaim the name of *The Most High God* in their heart, mind, voice, actions, and culture consciously or unconsciously. *YHWH or Yahweh* [Yah] is God to the Hebrew Israelites, *Theos* is the Greek word for God, *'Ĕlāhā or Alaha* is to Aramaic, French is to *Dieu*, Spanish is to *Dios*, *Nyame* is to the Akan (Twi) of Ghana, Italian is to *Dio*, Dutch is to *Godt*, *Allah* is to all Arabic speaking countries, German is to *Gott*, *Chineke* is to Igbo of Nigeria, Danish is to *Gud*, English is to *God*, and et al.

The *God consciousness* is also witnessed throughout various world religions, beliefs and practices in the likes of the Messianic, Christianity, Sumerians or Annunaki,

Judaism, Buddhism, Sun Worshippers, Hinduism, Islam,

Sikhism, Jainism, Taoism, Zoroastrianism, Atheism,

Shinto, Agnosticism, Confucianism, Polytheism, Wicca,

Monotheism, Unitarian, Universalism, Thelema, Satanism,

Animism, Spiritualism, Shamanism, Mind-body dualism,

various types of Traditional African beliefs, Hare Krishna,

Humanism, Atheist, Theist, Occultism, et al. Do not

confuse the *difference* between the *"God Consciousness"*

and the *"believe"* in the existence of *The Most High God*. I

do understand that there are some religious groups that

possess both the *"God Consciousness"* and the *"believe"*

in *The Most High God*. Interestingly, hundred percent of

mankind's religious groups and beliefs known and

unknown to some of us possess the *"God Consciousness"*

consciously or unconsciously but some of these groups

struggle to *"believe"* in the existence of *The Most High

God* although none of these religious groups and beliefs

categorically *deny* the existence of *The Most High God*. Most of the people who do not believe in the existence of *The Most High God*; hold that position because they claim that they cannot "prove" the actual existence of *The Most High God*. The fact of the matter is that *The Most High God's* existence requires no proof.

My question to you at this moment is, what really distinguish your justified *beliefs* from your *opinions*? Could your belief in science or religion be justified in my view as just an opinion and vice versa? What is knowledge in something? Can knowledge in/about something be limited, controlled, indoctrinated or brainwashed? Could one's love for knowledge be influenced by favoritism of one's culture, religion or tradition? The answer to the above questions is, *yes*. Now, what is passion for knowledge? Could an acquired knowledge be unlearned to relearn? Does one's culture, social environment (war, colonization, slavery) and traditions affect the teachings of knowledge? What is freedom? Can you be under the law and be free at the same time? Could one's skin color affect his/her freedom and the type of knowledge him/her is exposed to? What is truth? What is false? How can you differentiate between what is true and what is not true? Could the type of family and religious belief one is born into affect the way he/she believes? Who is *The Most High God*? Is *The Most High God* a human being sitting on a throne? Can humans limit who *The Most High God* is? Could fear affect one's ability to believe in God? Why does the thought of *The Most High God* make one feel somewhat comfortable or uncomfortable? Could *The Most High God* be everything or anything (*such as all types/kinds of energy, Light, Power, Force, Air, Fire, Water, literally everything or anything*)? These are some of the very few questions out of the many under the auspices of *epistemology* in relation to this subject matter. I want you to meditate on them and have a personal introspective analysis through your meditation.

With all the world's religious beliefs, cultures and traditions in perspective; it is safe to say that they are all in the quest to finding the answer(s) to how life began on earth, mankind's purpose on earth, and the very famous one, what happens after we die? One of the main motives consciously or unconsciously within the scientific world, mathematics, physics, astronomy, archaeology, and all the various studies has been about finding answers to the questions aforementioned. Our human inabilities to render answers to these questions oscillate many egos promulgating doubt to the logical reasoning of the existence of *The Most High God*. Hence, waiting for science or another human to discover or find *The Most High God* as one finds a missing cell phone is shallow. *The Most High God* is far vast than mankind's porous ego. Once again, *The Most High God* is a *spirit* and only those on a spiritual level can connect with *The Most High God*.

On the next page, I will use some diagrams to explain further about the *"God Consciousness"* in everything. I hope that this adds additional clarity to the unspoken awareness of *The Most High God*'s presence in our culture, thoughts, ideas, expressions of appreciations, language, history, and the likes of many.

Okay, let's turn to the next page and get started.

The "God Consciousness" In Everything Diagrammatic summary.

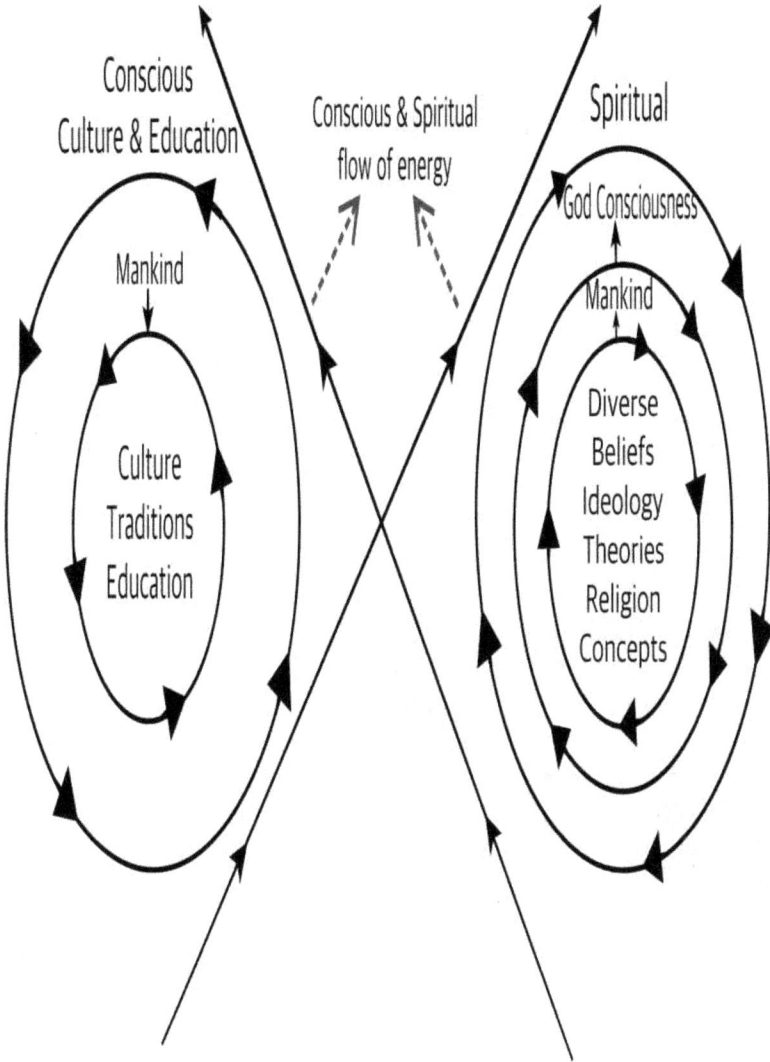

Conscious Culture & Education

Conscious & Spiritual flow of energy

Spiritual

God Consciousness

Mankind

Mankind

Culture
Traditions
Education

Diverse
Beliefs
Ideology
Theories
Religion
Concepts

Fig.2

The "God Consciousness" in everything may come to few or many as complicatedly intertwining, however; it's uniform in its energetic flow. The blur in its possible confusion lies in its clarity through a spiritual dive of one's self (requires *spiritual mindset*). One giveaway is that, no matter where you stand from a conscious perspective. There is a gut feeling of clarity in oneness of all beings in the universe. This is a taste of the "God Consciousness" in everything.

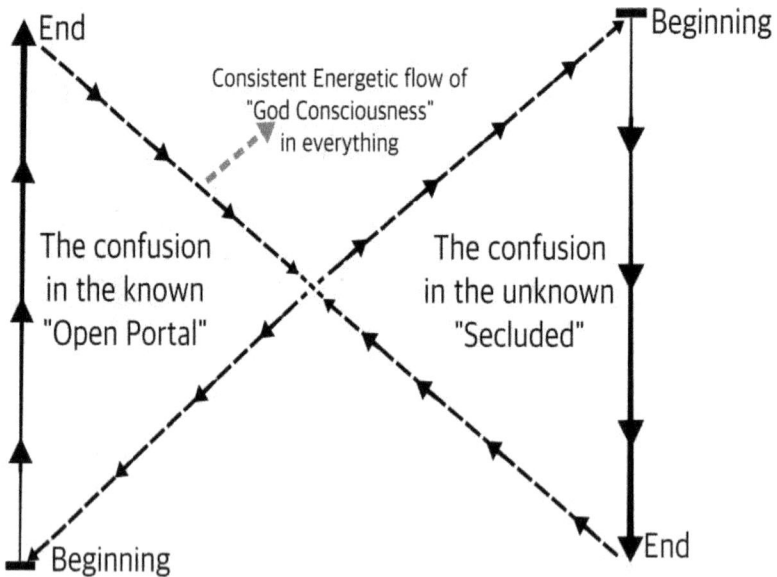

End

Beginning

Consistent Energetic flow of "God Consciousness" in everything

The confusion in the known "Open Portal"

The confusion in the unknown "Secluded"

Beginning

End

Fig.3

Think about these Rhetorical Logics

❖ How can the concept, ideas, practices, and beliefs of *The Most High God* exist throughout the universe, galaxies, languages, dialects, cultures, traditions, folktales, literally everything (pre, during, mid, current, and future) if *The Most High God* doesn't truly exist?

❖ Why doesn't science have a *one hundred percent solid answer* to <u>how</u> our world began and <u>why</u> did it begin in the first place? <u>What</u> intelligent being/force/energy/light with respect to science caused the big bang to erupt? <u>*How were things existing in this intelligence's realm and time prior*</u> to everything and can science *one hundred percent prove it*? <u>*Were*</u> there *intelligent beings* existing prior to the existence of our world, universe and everything in it?

❖ How can mankind create a duplicate "god" (smaller gods) if the original "*Most High God*" doesn't exist? Ponder very well on this question.

❖ How is *time measured* in *the spiritual realm* if science doesn't have the tool to function in the spiritual realm? Can science categorically prove that *time is relative in the spiritual realm* or that *there is "no time" (time being of no relevance)* in essence of *the spiritual realm*?

❖ If mankind continue to fight over the peripheral things, such as: hair type, skin color, racism, and all the *punk* things that cause division and hate among ourselves then how insolent of anyone to slightly attempt to debunk the existence of *The Most High God*.

We all have the mandate to execute some research to find some answers to *why we die physically* and *what happens after we die*. Humans cannot necessarily be in existence just to be born, eat, grow, work, and then die. Just like that

and after death to say it all ends is just a lazy way to bow

out in intellectual shame. To sit aloof from researching,

enlightenment, or knowledge of the existence of God is

simply to be lazy, confused and living a life with no

purpose. The "feeling", "voice" and "gut" that persuades

you to believe that you "live" beyond this physical realm is

a voice to reckon. Let that voice be your guide and

motivation to draw you close to your *true source*, which is

spiritual from *The Most High God.*

CHAPTER 4

God's Audacity: The Logic of God's Existence.

CHAPTER 4

THE THEORY OF GOD'S CORE

Our single purpose to one another and the planet is to love one another and to love the planet we live on or call home. The other part to our purpose is our spiritual love for *The Most High God, The Creator*. Our life on this physical planet, our interaction with each other, what we do and how we do it have its solution in *love*. What is the universal advice leaders, career advisors, religious leaders, counselors, and parents give when one is stuck on finding what to do with their life? 99.99% of the time, you are advised to find *something you love*, work on that *thing you love* with passion, get the right training or learn about *"what you love"* and go for it to win it with all you've got. We come across such advice in almost every aspect of our lives, be it marriage, career, college, finding love, et al. Also, when you are in dismay and feel like you are selling yourself short; you are advised to love yourself enough to take care of yourself. We take care of ourselves by resting, checking our mental health, getting out of unhealthy situation and the likes. All in all, love seems to be the core to our being and whenever we are off-balance, we are advised to get back to the basics of love; our core.

It is out of *love* that everything exist (both known and unknown to mankind). It was out of *love* that everything came into existence and it would be out of *love* that everything would be put back in order. Absolutely nothing can exist *fully* without *love*. *Love* will always be *love* regardless of the energy surrounding it. I came up with what I call the *"Theory of God's Core"* which is *Love*. The diagram shown below is meant to expand on the *"Theory of God's Core"*. Pay close attention to the flow and direction of the arrows.

Fig.4

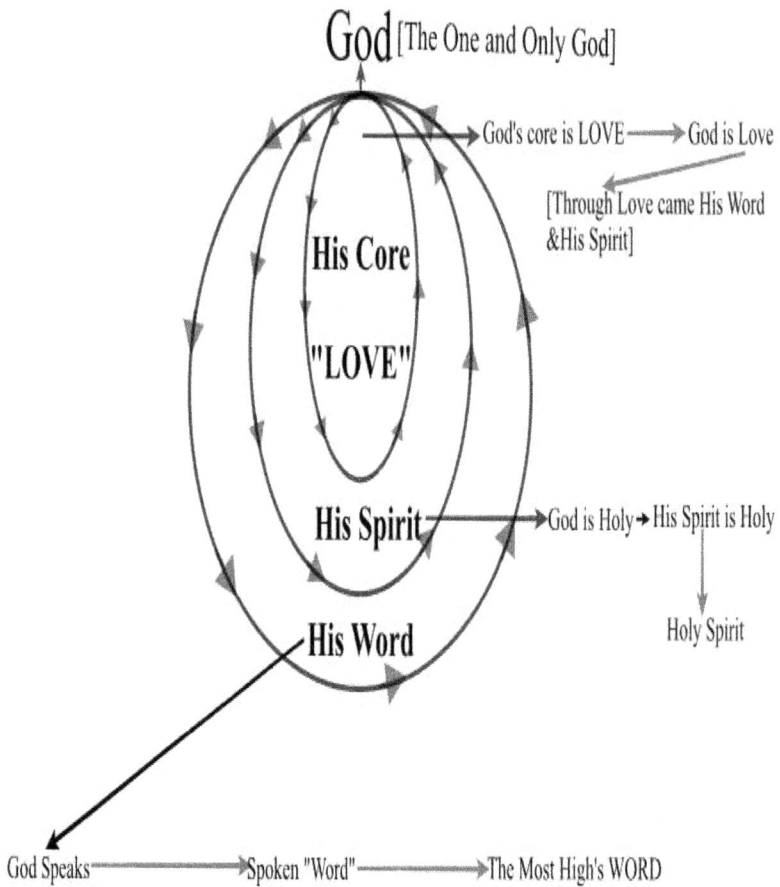

God [The One and Only God]

God's core is LOVE → God is Love

[Through Love came His Word &His Spirit]

His Core

"LOVE"

His Spirit → God is Holy → His Spirit is Holy

His Word

Holy Spirit

God Speaks → Spoken "Word" → The Most High's WORD

Love manifested in the *"Flesh"* is *The Most High's*

Creations. The *Spoken Word* of *The Most High God* was

the means to all existence and creations known and

53

unknown to mankind. _Love_ manifested in the _"Spirit"_ is the "Holy Spirit". Let me break it down a little further, _Love_ _"saves"_ and _'teaches"_. To _save_ is to rescue or to deliver. _The Most High God's_ name is "YHWH" (a short form of His full name "Yahweh", Yhwh [Hebrew]). The statement I am about to make is very important and you would need to understand its meaning; _The Most High God's "Word"_ is _"The Most High's Word"_. To _"teach"_ is to counsel, the _Holy Spirit_ of _The Most High, The Creator_ is a counselor, to inspire, direct, comfort, convict, et al). As humans, we know that contumacious individuals face chastisement and are reprimanded. This is all done out of _love_ with the intent to discipline and ethically correct the wrong. Mankind consciously or unconsciously replicates the concept of _love_ in our communities, societies, governments, various institutions, and on a micro level within our homes/families.

The diagram below details how everything known and unknown to mankind was initiated/manifested/spoken into existence/life by *The Most High God* through *His Core (Love)*:   **Fig.5**

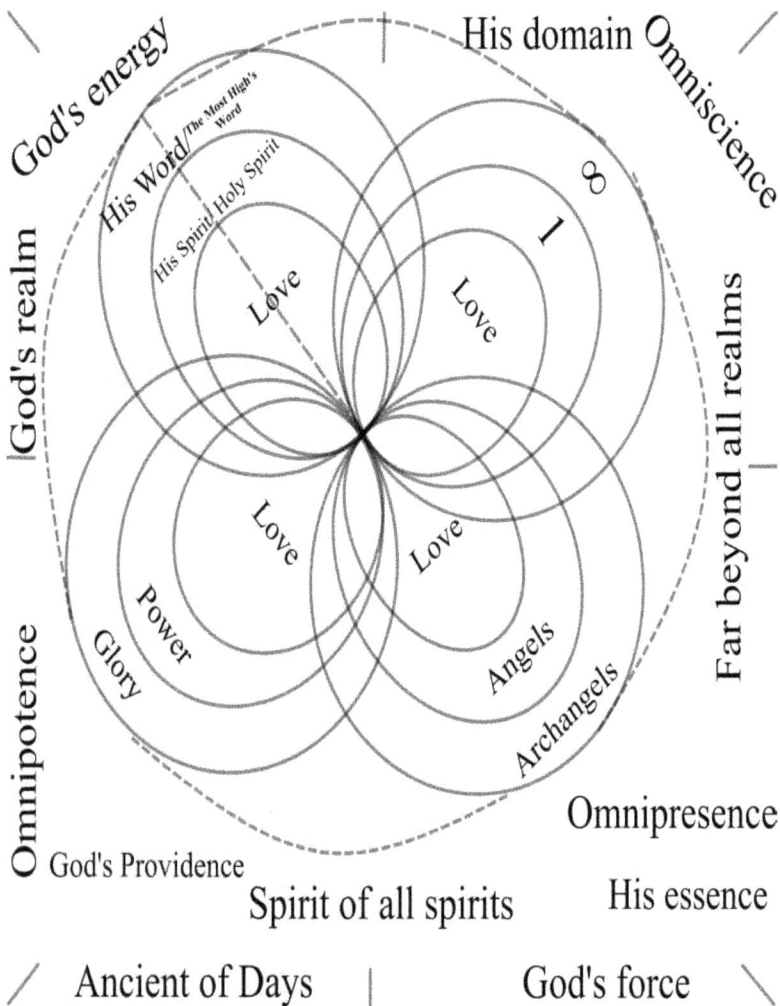

THE CONSCIOUSNESS and UNCONSCIOUSNESS OF HUMANS EXHIBITING "THE CORE OF GOD" a.k.a (LOVE).

Within the human and material realm, the "God Core" a.k.a (Love) comes to play when the "*giver*" and the "*receiver*" share the *same intended outcome of energy* considered as good, holy, happy, loving, exciting, positive, or satisfaction. *Love* is always the reason for our actions (good or bad). Misunderstanding and miseducation of *love's* characteristic entity cause great suffering in the universe. We need to get back to *love's* origin in order to truly understand it. Whenever the *intended outcome of energy* differs from the *giver* and the *receiver*; there tend to be chaos everywhere. It must take an reassessment of "*love*" in order for things to return to its normal state. *Love* has been the reason why some nations even go to war. The soldiers profess the *"love"* for their country with *different energy outcome* (casualties, economic collapse) intended to the *"receiver"* -which is the other country at war. *Love* is also the reason why we marry, have children, have acquaintances and definitely one of the reasons to protect oneself or family members.

With respect to the *"Theory of God's Core"*, the entire human body is full of different kinds of energy; at the *core* of it all, is *"love"*. *Love* is the *core* of every energy. Whenever negative energy surrounds *love* due to the corruption of the *"intent"* exerted by negative energy; it yields deadly, unwarranted pain, anger, discomfort, destruction, heartbreak and torture. The negative energy is repelled by the *"Energy of Repellant"* that shields the *core*, which is *"love"* from any corruption. It is mutually exclusive for the *"giver"* to have a *selfish "intent"* which was corrupted by the *"energy" of selfishness* and deliver a

loving effect to the *"receiver"* and vice versa.

The *"Theory of God's Core"* is solidly engrained at the heart/center of our *spirit* (our true form). The human spirit belongs to *The Most High God* and *He* has complete sovereignty over the human *spirit (your life, God's breath, God breathed into you to become a living soul)*. The figure below exhibits the general flow of the *"Theory of God's Core"* within every human: **Fig6**.

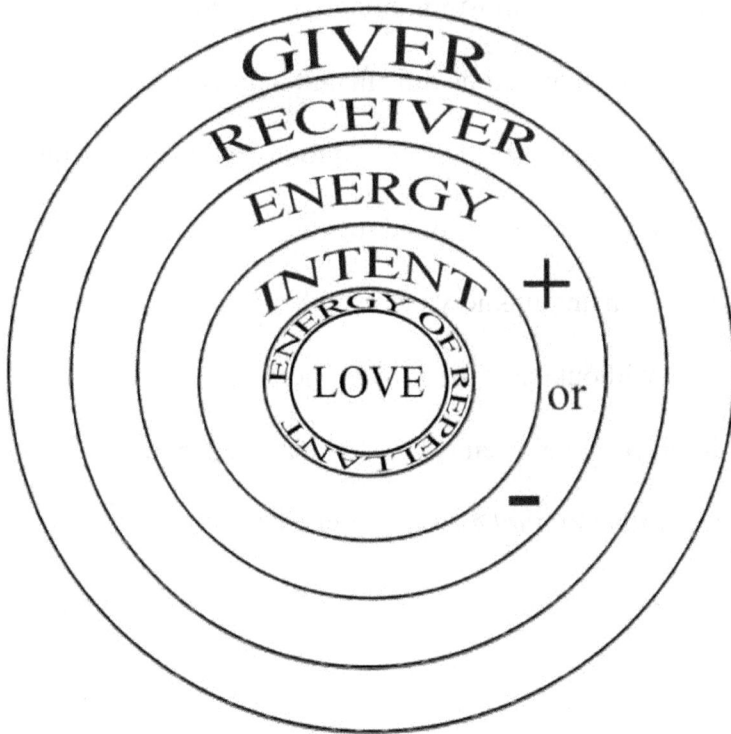

The *energy of repellant* is only attracted to *positive "intent"* which is initiated by a *positive energy.* This is because *The Most High God* repels anything that is unrighteous (negative energy).

Self-affirmations exert *positive energy* which triggers *positive intent* piercing through the *energy of repellant* to the *core of your being.* Self-love is as important to your consciousness and most importantly your spirit as the *energy of air* that you breathe in and out every microsecond. *Love* is the solution to everything happening within our universe. Mankind together with every living spirit known and unknown to us will eventually self-destruct without exercising *love.* The figure below shows the interaction between two individuals reflecting a *mutual energy* with a *mutual expected* outcome.

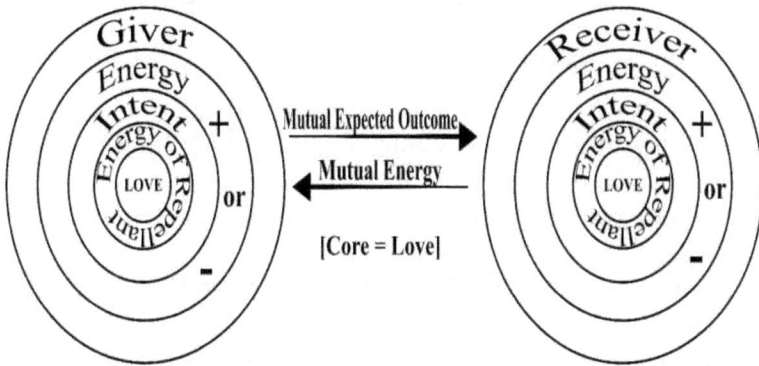

Fig.7

Even the craziest, meanest, and most dangerous individuals possess *love* (because this is the *core* of our *spirit*). They act the way they do because they are disconnected from their *core* due to *recurring negative energy* corrupting their *intent* (could be: fear, anger, hate, deception, pride, loss of a loved one, revenge, insecurities, et al). Unless an individual is directly connected to his/her *core* on both micro and macro level, he/she will forever be a lost soul.

Such people are toxic to the environment, destructive and chaotic to everywhere they go. They sow seeds of discord and deception to those that are spiritually delusional and suffering from similar disconnect. If you do not know what happens to you after you die, if you doubt who you are, if you consistently feel inadequate, unloved, and consistently confused about your purpose on this planet then you are simply disconnected from your *core* (the very foundation of your true self).

I am going to outline an alternative breakdown of the *"Theory of God's Core"* within every human. This outline will constitute some day to day human emotions, interactions, actions and exhibitions that we consciously or unconsciously may be aware or unaware of under the sun.

ILLUSTRATION

Energy [+ or -]

A.   GIVER ----------------------------------→RECEIVER

Core is Love

GIVER ←---------------------------------- RECEIVER

This is the resting phase of the *"Theory of God's Core"* (Love) within mankind with balanced state of inertia when there is no movement, action or communication initiated or ongoing between the *giver* and the *receiver*.

Energy [+] exerted by the giver/initiator

B.   GIVER --------------------------------→RECEIVER

Core is Love

GIVER: Exerting *positive energy* with *positive intent* to the *receiver*. The *giver* exhibits an *intent* of <u>excitement</u> and <u>kindness</u> (positive energy).

RECEIVER: Positively feels thankful but somehow wonder if there is/are any commitment(s) attached since *no action/work* was put into place to *render* such *positive energy* from the *giver*.

Energy [+] exerted by the giver/initiator

C. GIVER ----------------------------------→RECEIVER

Core is Love

←--**Energy [+] contained by <u>receiver</u> with mutual expectation** ----

GIVER: Exerts *positive energy* with *positive intent* with prior communication and agreement with the *receiver.*

RECEIVE: Feeling of excitement, *positive energy.* In this case, *receiver* puts in work/action. He or She is expecting the *agreed upon* reward/compensation from the *giver.* There is a *"positive mutual"* expectation and outcome between the *giver* and *receiver.* When this happens, the *receiver* and the *giver* are both satisfied and appreciative of each other (the outcome).

Energy [-] exerted by the giver/initiator

D. GIVER ----------------------------------→RECEIVER

Core is Love

GIVER: Exerts *negative energy* with *negative intent.* The *giver* is feeling his *corrupt intent* pumped with *negative emotions* of adrenalin to incite pain, hurt, deception, heartbreak, loss, disaster, chaos to the *receiver.* In this case, the *receiver* is unaware of the *giver's* intent.

RECEIVER: Unexpectedly gets hit with the *negative energy* from the *giver.* The *receiver* is unprepared, unaware and caught by surprise in a toxic, unfriendly and weird situation. The *receiver* is *negatively* affected, hurt, in pain, possible loss of something dear to him/her, possible death in some cases, et al.

NOTE: In life or death situations, although the *receiver* is unaware and unprepared for the *giver's negative energy*; the *receiver* is able to react quickly in an attempt to save himself/herself. Such as **self-defense cases**, the fight or flight instinct of *intent* may kick in aiding the *receiver* to respond in a swift way to save his or her life due to the *energy of self-love* within all of us.

63

Energy [-] exerted by the giver/initiator

E.   GIVER ----------------------------------→RECEIVER

Core is Love

←--<u>Energy [-]</u> contained by <u>receiver</u> with mutual expectation-----

 GIVER: Exerts *negative energy* with *negative intent* to hurt, destroy the *receiver*. Tension has been brewing between the *giver* and the *receiver*; both parties are aware of the possibility of emotional explosions that can render some serious repercussions.

RECEIVER: Aware of the *negative energy* from the *receiver* and aware of the possibility of emotional explosions that can cause severe damage, hurt, pain to both of them. *Receiver* tend to also prepare for the possible outcome. In this case, both parties possess *mutual energy* and *mutually know or understand* the *possible outcome*.

NOTE: *Negative energy* has no place within the *"Theory of God's Core"* a.k.a *Love* due to the *Energy of Repellant* repelling all the *negativity*. The *Energy of Repellant* functions this way due to the positivity and holiness of *The Most High God*. Hence, e*very negative energy* with *corrupt intent* initiated by the soul/consciousness will only destroy himself or herself if such *negative energy* isn't quenched with the spirit of *love*.

The harmonious flow of the epitomized *"Theory of God's Core"* embedded in mankind's *DNA* is only at play when the *giver* and the *receiver* are in a *mutually positive energy* flow of *intent*. The obvious thing happening among the human populace is that, both the *giver* and the *receiver* act on the basis of *love* under *different* circumstances, influences and intentions. In situations such as when you are in love but your actions are not out of love, war with another country, civil war, ethnic war, and "war" in general, bribery and corrupt power (corruption), self-hate, greed, et al. Regardless of the outside or inside influences; for there to be an experience of the *"Theory of God's Core"*, the *heart* and the *mind* must be at an *inseparable interlocking conformity* with one another through *pure unification* of *love* and *positive intent* exhibited by both the *giver* and the *receiver*.

In summary:

- ✓ The *intent* is always initiated by the *giver/initiator*.

- ✓ The *intent* can either be polluted or kept in its true state (pure) depending on the kind/type of energy the *giver/initiator* chooses with his/her *Free Will*.

- ✓ The *energy* represents our *daily choices*. Everything around us physically and spiritually are all different kinds of energy.

- ✓ The <u>core</u> (Love) also known as the *"Theory of God's Core"* never change no matter the magnitude of the *negative energy* and *negative intent* outside its *core*. The *core* always remains pure.

- ✓ The *receiver* in most cases suffer the most since the *receiver* mostly do not *initiate* the *energy (negative or positive)* and the *intent*.

- ✓ The *giver* is punished in cases of severe damage to the *receiver* in accordance to the existing or established law.

✓ The mutuality of the *positive energy* and *intent* exerted by both the *giver* and *receiver* is the only way to trigger the natural flow and experience of the *"Theory of God's Core"* in life.

CHAPTER 5

CHAPTER 5

TYPES OF SPIRITUAL CONSCIOUSNESS IN RELATION TO *THE LOGIC OF GOD'S EXISTENCE*.

Humans are not the only conscious creatures within the realms of ∞ and **1**(all created things). Intelligence is measured differently in every realm. Your awareness of the human consciousness is only magnified when connected to the *source*, **X** (*The Most High, The Omniscient*). It is laughable to think that humans are on their own in this universe and that atomic and nuclear bombs are the way to go. World leaders and governments are weaponizing almost everything from our food to air, waters and some secret massive biological weapons. I can tell you this, from a conscious level; mankind is dealing with things that do not have earthly bodies. These things are demons, principalities, things that do not look like humans or relate to anything human. Mankind's solution is to reconnect their mind or most importantly their *"true selves"* (spiritual being) to *The Most High*. Let me ask you this rhetorical question, what is primitive in terms of conscience? God created so many things with high consciousness including the angels and other spirits that travel a trillionth times faster than the speed of light. We are all *spiritual energies* and as such very powerful to the point that even the *super gamma rays* cannot be matched to our power. Once again, humans need to re-connect to the *true source*, which is *The Most High, All-Powerful intelligence, Omnipotent, Spirit of all spirits and the Energy of all energies.*

On a human level, the *conscious energy* known as *"consciousness"* is simply within our earthly body. Our body is just a package that comes in different sizes, shapes and complexion (due to melanin). The important aspect of our being is the *consciousness (both spiritual and soul)*

71

contained within our earthly body. Every living thing

houses some sort of consciousness, that's what makes a

living thing a living thing.

As a living person full of *consciousness,* I am not a:
*Christian or Catholic– *Sun worshippers who worship on*

Sunday.

*Muslim.

*Jewish.

*Hinduist.

*Agnostic.

*Atheist.

*Or any form of world religion.

Because:

* *The Most High, The Creator* do not have a religion.

The Most High is not a Christian – fact (The term
"Christian" is pagan in ancient Rome as Mithras followers).

*I believe in the true God who's *The Most High, The
Creator* of everything in existence known and unknown to
mankind.

*I believe and follow the *Torah* and the *Old Testaments.*

*I am free to relate, communicate, fellowship and worship
The Most High, The Creator directly.

Let me share a little experience with you, I wake up every day feeling like wisdom is flowing through me like a fountain of infinite water deriving from a melanated genesis. I live, I breathe, I am "being". I am intricately in uniformity with everything that has existed, is existing and that which is unequivocally yet to come. It is inexplicably grand, royal and bona fide to all existence and nonexistence. The source of everything revealed to few and anonymous to many due to their spiritual deafness and cavernous tranquilized sleep. The source of every intelligence and wisdom originate from *The Most High*. Now, let's transition to *physical consciousness. Physical consciousness* is when your brain sees the world for what it is *only* at its physical state. The human eye is just a window of lens for the brain to interpret the physical things in our environment. The *"seat" of consciousness* (located within the brain) triggers *full vision* of our consciousness. This helps us to react accordingly to the physical object (*ie: fire, tree, food, sun, houses, roads, cars, computers, money, books, animals, et al*) translated by the brain. The physical eye is just a reflective object with which the energy of light passes through. From there, the energy of light is diverted and distributed to the brain which is in charge of "sight". We cannot see with our physical eye if our brain is dead, but we can see with our brain with or without the physical eye. Since the brain houses the *soul*, it is connected to the *spirit (our true self)* in a supernaturally undetectable form of energetic frequency implanted and supremely orchestrated by *The Most High, The Creator*.

Absolutely no one in existence, be it physical or spiritual has the ability to touch the human *spirit*. It is *for* and *belongs* to the one and only *Most High, The Great I AM, Omnipotence, Omnipresence, Omniscient, Holiest Holiness, Eternal Super Hypernova Radiant Preeminent Energy, Spirit of all spirits, Light of all lights, Force of all forces, The Source of everything* known and unknown to

every creation.

The Four (4) Types of Spiritual Consciousness in Relation to The Logic of God's Existence.

I hope that by now, you are aware that every human is a *spirit* at the *core*. Our true self is not physical, death is just the spiritual "door" to exit from this physical domain to the spiritual realm. In this book, we will look at the four types of *spiritual consciousness* in creation. These are the four types of *spiritual consciousness* in direct relation to our spiritual awareness: *unconscious spirituality, unconscious-conscious spirituality, conscious spirituality, and conscious-conscious spirituality.*

The Unconscious Spirituality: This is

someone who is unconscious in relation to spiritual awareness. This individual is *spiritually unaware* of what is true, lies, facts, fake or real. The *unconscious spirituality* lives only by the *"bread"*. Whatever gives the physical body comfort, peace and livability is good for him or her regardless of the means at which the needs in question was attained. This is what I call *spiritual comatose*. This person is in a tranquilized sleep so deep to the point that he or she has no spiritual connection. Inertly confused and questions everything about *The Most High*. He or She is unwilling to execute his or her own research to find answers to the spiritual insensate state of being. The character of his or her insentience denial in relation to *The Most High* deceives him or her to think that he or she is wise but in actuality, a fool in the eyes of *The Most High*.

The Unconscious-Conscious Spirituality:

This is the individual that is either *consciously* or *unconsciously unaware* of his or her *spiritual unconsciousness*. This individual takes one step forward in a spiritual quest to finding some facts about *The Most High* but then takes four steps back from where he or she started.

This individual is easily manipulated in deception by various influences of religion. He or She believes various lies packaged with indoctrination, narrow mindedness and dogmatic religious traditions that has nothing to do with *The Most High*. Instead of spiritually depending on *The Most High* and seeking *His* ways; this individual rather makes the physical human or a physical entity (physical images) his or her "go-to" point of contact as a means to get to *The Most High*. The *unconscious-conscious* puts his or her belief, trust, and faith in almost everything he or she receives from his or her physical "go-to" point of contact.

The Conscious Spirituality: This individual

is epistemologically *compos mentis* in the physical realm. He or she sees the material world for what it is and nothing else. This person has not *fully* transcended spiritually due to his or her conflict between the knowledge of this material world and the knowledge within the spiritual world.

This person is alert, aware of past events, current events and future events. He or She is on a spiritual journey to fully discover the necessary spiritual tools to *fully* transcend. This individual like to read, research, and ask questions to things he or she doesn't know or understand. This individual is positively sentient with an inspired determination to know himself or herself in regard to origination, purpose here on earth and the afterlife.

The Conscious-Conscious Spirituality: This

person lives *spiritually* with great pious to *The Most High.* He or She has transcended through the material realm. They comprehend things within the spiritual realm and practice all the inspirations and directions from *The Most High.* This individual teaches, inspires, enlightens and trains others to discover their *spiritual wholeness*. He or She is not perturbed by physical events happening within the physical realm. He or She seeks wisdom over material things because he/she understands the difference between these two energies (physical and spiritual). This person tends to be on a high energy level of spiritual consciousness. Seeks purity with an aptitude to easily break down the most tortuous labyrinthine things both in the physical and spiritual realm.

Where do you see yourself? What level of consciousness do you think you are on currently? Are you ready and willing to embark on a spiritual journey if you are not already on one? Remember, this is a personal decision. You ought to consciously decide to connect with *The Most High* through application of your *Free Will*. The spiritual journey is individualistic. You cannot rush or compete because things of the spirit in relation to *The Most High* are managed, directed, instructed and taught by the *Spirit* of *The Most High*. At the end of our earthly days, we will all find out about our true destiny. So why not invest your time and energy into researching, learning and educating yourself about your eternal life instead of

choosing to fully invest your time and energy into your

short time life on this physical realm called earth.

Check out Fig.8 on the next page for the

diagrammatic exhibition of spiritual consciousness.

Diagrammatic exhibition of spiritual consciousness

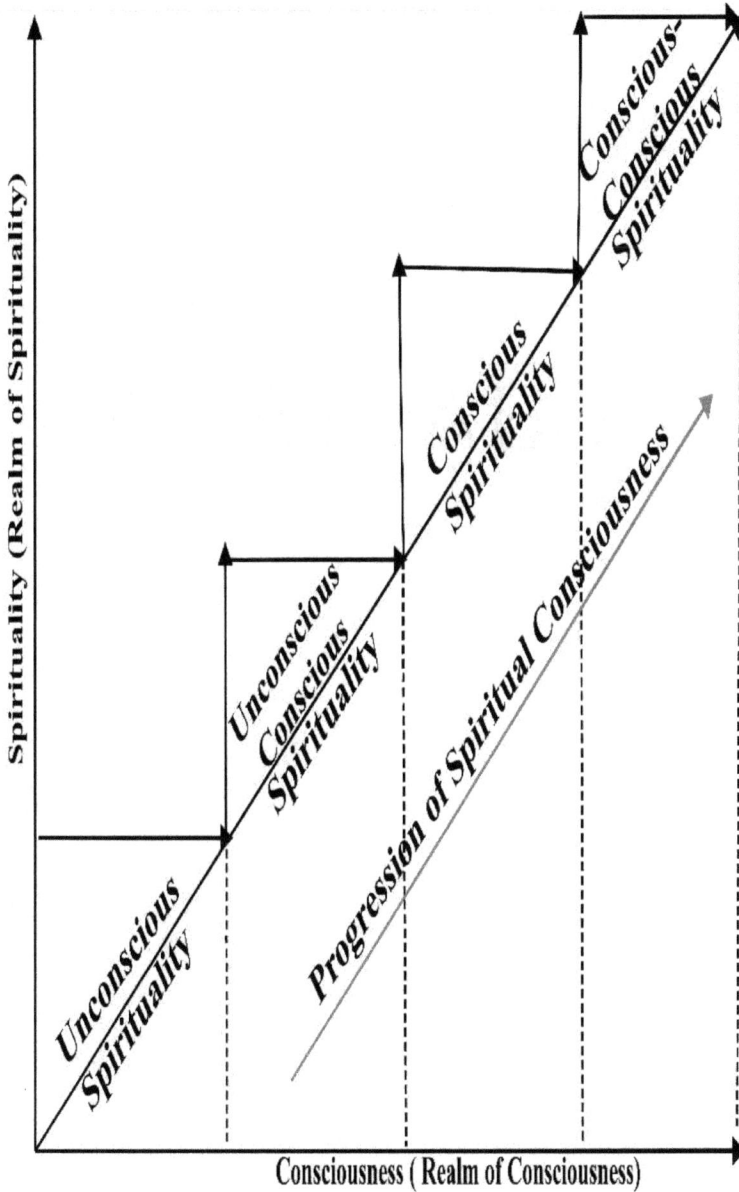

Fig.8

CHAPTER 6

CHAPTER 6

SPIRITS, SOULS, LIVING THINGS and NON-LIVING THINGS.

God is the *Spirit of all spirits*. There is the *Holy spirit*, *The Most High's* **Word** and the *Spirit of Spirits* (which is *God, The Creator, Omnipotent, Omnipresent, Omniscient*). *The Most High's* creations are *His* physical representations according to proper hierarchy. *The Most High* can never be physically touched or held because *The Most High* doesn't have a physical body. *The Most High* is simply everything, hyper-supernova electromagnetic energy, and literally everything known and unknown to mankind. *The Most High* can be anything and everything He chooses to be. As the Spirit of all spirits, *He* can take the shape and form of literally anything. Man cannot limit the magnitude of *The*

Most High. Many men and women have unconsciously attempted and continue to misinterpret the power of *The Most High* and *His* being to just something convenient to their imagination, comprehension and sometimes societal influence. *The Most High* is bigger, greater and powerful beyond measure.

I would like to emphatically emphasize again that, *The Most High* is not human. God doesn't have a body or a figure but can take the shape of any object that pleases *Him*. *The Most High* does not have sex classification (male or female). It is important to state that, the usage of "*He*" when talking about *The Most High*, *The Creator* is a language and culture instituted by *The Most High* through *His* creations. This could be seen in how records from the bible were written as well as other world cultures and religion with diverse languages exhibiting this uniformity. Since *The Most High* is the *Spirit of all spirits*; that simply translates that all *His* creations are spirits. We are obviously different kinds of energies possessed by *The Most High* alone. In the simplest term, *The Most High* is the source.

Let me share this truth with you, every human being is a "spirit" living in an earthly uniform(body). Every living organism possesses a "soul' including plants (Don't get lost here - follow my narrative). The *"God form"* is the highest form. The *spiritual form* is the next including angels and demons *(fallen angels)*. Humans fully become spirits (without our earthly bodies) right after our body is detached (when deceased). The spirit and soul (memories, consciousness) are both detached from the earthly body upon death. Hence the *human spirit* has memories (that was the *"being"* when the *human spirit* was living within the earthly body). Some intellectuals are attesting that science can now steal one's consciousness. One thing for sure is that science can never touch the *"spirit"* of humans which is the true *"you"*. I will go deeper into this topic about science in the next chapter. Spirits constituting the human spirits, demons or fallen angels cannot ascend to *The Most High's* realm without *His* permission. For a diagrammatic reference on this specific point of discussion, check out Fig.1 in Chapter 2.

Mankind is directly connected to the basic foundation of spiritual life either consciously or unconsciously. Spirit or spiritual essence is also known as *Energy*. **Human's** comprehension of energy is part of the reason why the money we all use to buy, and sell is known as *Currency*. Take a quick seven seconds pause to think about why we all know money as *Currency* worldwide. What is the etymological and scientific definition of *Currency?* What is the expanded meaning of *Currency*? What is its derivative, source or origination? Is it not from *Current?* Now, what is *Current? Current* is simply *"energy"* used or existing in the past, present, and yet to be used (future). *Current* cannot be destroyed in any fashion no matter how hard we try. *Current* is free and flows through its own circulation.

Current reacts differently to different *current*. Hence, the ideology to use money or you lose it (that is when the *Currency or "Current"* becomes docile or unused). *Currency* can be anything mankind gives/grants *power* to as a means to *buy* and *sell*. Currency can be paper based, item based, or minerals based. At the end of the day, it all depends on the *energetic power* that humans render to something as a means to trade.

Current ------------------→ Currency -----------→ Money

Negative – or Positive + charge.	**"in Circulation"**	Symbol.
Energy, Motion, Flow,	**"Exchange" "In Usage".**	Physical
Supply of energy.	**Medium, Converter,**	Representation
Used, Recycled, Now, Present,	**Electronic.**	Could be Gold,
Future.	**Acceptable means to**	Coins, Bank
High, Low, Alternate,	***buy & sell.***	Notes, Salt,
Direct forms of Energy.		et al.

Money, in the illustration above could be literally anything acceptable by those in power/rulership on this physical planet. When we apply the philosophy of common sense through logic; we would be intrigued to discover that everything in the universe is connected to the flow of *Current* (which is *energy*). Everything in the universe is simply *Energy:* love, emotions, feelings, air, sun, water, kindness, food, trees, fishes, plants, every animal both on land and in water, excitement, anger, success, unity, diversity, education, light, day, night, et al.

Fig.9

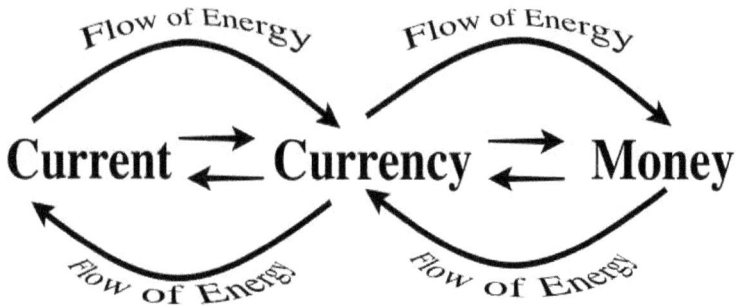

Flow of Energy · Flow of Energy

Current ⇄ Currency ⇄ Money

Flow of Energy · Flow of Energy

Those in power and influence have only tried to use physical representations to represent very few of the energies existing in our universe. This is because we are not familiar with the complete works of the universe. Majority of us have little to no understanding of the *Oneness* of the universe. There is even a struggle for clarity and specificity among the very few who may have the slightest comprehension of it due to our reliance on our own understanding instead of seeking wisdom and guidance from *The Most High, The Creator*. Examine Fig.3

Oneness with the universe before examining Fig.10 for

better comprehension:

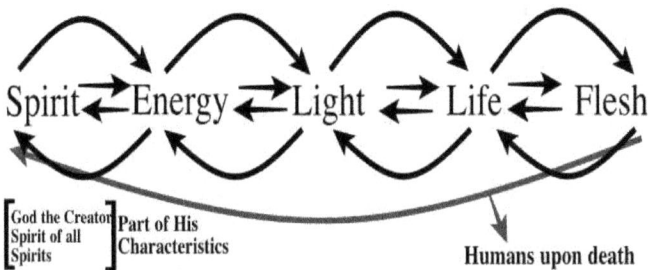

Fig.10

Being in the *Flesh* is consciousness through awareness to

our earthly environment. We record everything that

happens here, and we are able to relate to one another

consciously knowing that we are all human. When another

human fail to relate to another human on a "*socially*

acceptable" manner; other humans within that culture or

community say that "*you have no soul*". In other terms, you

are not *conscious* of another human being with the *same*

right and *characteristics* as every human. Our *soul* aids us to survive on earth (material universe). That is why in some materialistic situations our *true self* (the *spirit*) struggles/wrestles with the *soul* (*consciousness*) on things relating to our true origin, *The Most High*.

The *energies* contained in animals are of different form or type comparable to humans. Mankind consume the physical representations of different kinds of energies contained within plants, trees, animals (both on land and in water), insects and all kinds of *physical* living things. The *physical representations* of all living things are connected to the soil/dust/ground as well. Hence, every living thing eventually decompose in their physical state when the *energy* departs from their physical containers (body). That *energy* is simply transformed to its original state (the energy is not wasted, it doesn't die, it is eternal). Human beings are very special because we are the only physical representations that constitute direct "*air*" (different kind of *energy*) from *The Most High, The Creator*. The air/breath from *The Most High* is relevant in order for us(humans) to become *Living Souls* (awareness of the ground/earth/soil/, our environment, conscious, living, being alive). Humans are *The Most High's Breath of Fresh Air,* making our true source of being *spiritual*. Since the *breath* originated from the *Spirit of all spirits*, who is *The Most High*.

In a *physical* sense/state, humans *die* but in the *spiritual* sense/state; humans basically *transform* from *its current state* to *the actualization state* after *death*. Which is being a *spirit* without the earthly corruptible body. I want to swiftly speak to my readers who may be science fanatics, use the *energy* of self-control to tame your itch to question everything about *The Most High* until you read chapter 7 and apply the *energy* of wisdom to scientific reasoning. Do not be limited in your field of study/indoctrination. Science is a step stool to learning about aspects of *The Most High, The Creator*.

Our body is a power house full of energy to the extent that before the body "shuts down"; it uses all the *energy* stored within its muscles, veins, brain, and other tissues. For instance, when you are cold, before you freeze to death; the body consciously reacts to keep you warm as much as possible before it shuts itself down.

The figure (Fig.11) detail how *energy* flows through us and how we react to the flow of *energy* in our environment:

Fig.11

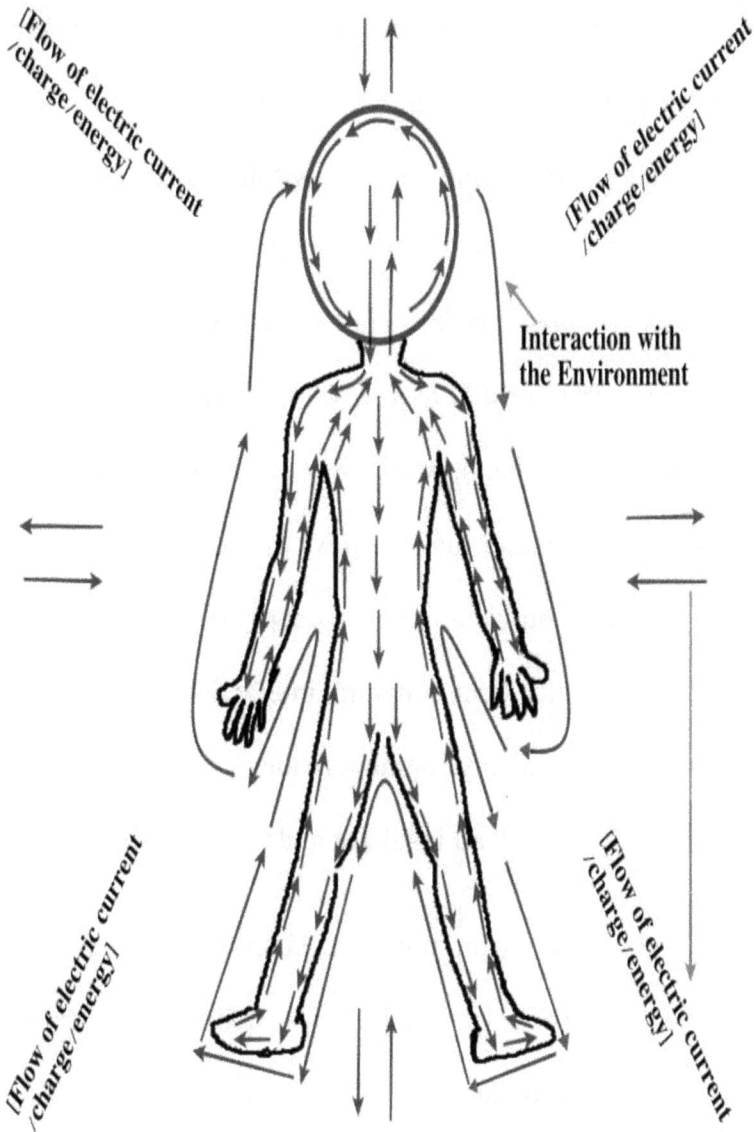

[Flow of electric current/charge/energy]

[Flow of electric current/charge/energy]

Interaction with the Environment

[Flow of electric current/charge/energy]

[Flow of electric current/charge/energy]

Our *words* and *actions* are all *energy*. The *spirit* within us exerts *positive energy* as the *body/flesh* exerts *negative energy*. *Equal exertions* from *both sides* are needed in order for us(humans) to function *morally* within our physical realm. *Spiritual disconnection* occurs if the *flesh's energy* outweighs the *spirit's energy* due to one's desire to *freely choose* through *Free Will* to *feed* the *flesh* more than the *spirit*. On the other hand, when the *spirit* is heavily *fed* to produce *energy* greater than the *flesh* then one becomes *more spiritual*. You would then be deeply *connected* to the *spiritual realm*. The body's natural interaction with its internal and external environment render it to possess the characteristics of both an insulator and a conductor.

Illustratively, when an individual is upset or irate, he/she is advised to calm down. We all check/monitor our *energy* flow through the conduct of *meditation*. Every culture, religion and ethnicities have their own way of *meditation*. We all need to check ourselves introspectively through *meditation* to welcome self and environmental awareness to our aura. *Meditation* helps us to *see*, *know* and *decide* on the *type of energy* we welcome into our lives or associate with in our environment. We are all advised to find a quiet place to *meditate*. It is definitely going to be *hard* to *meditate* at the heart of Manhattan with all the car traffics, noises, hustling and bustling of *energies* everywhere. The hustling and bustling are good for connection/connecting but contrary to "*recharging*", "*meditating*" or "*deep introspection*" which needs a quiet environment. Everything is simply *energy* flowing in its path of current. We are all *spirits (the highest form of energy)* in an earthly body. *Spirits* are simply made of *energy* (different kind of *energy*). There is *oneness* in the uniformity of all creatures on the *spiritual level.* Hence, *The Most High's* supreme audacity to bring everything to judgement.

THE DICHOTOMY OF THE SPIRIT AND SOUL

The *spirit* and the *soul* are two different entities residing within the human body. Read the creation story in any religion, culture, belief or tradition. There may be some slight difference(s) in how the creation story was passed on from posterity to posterity. However, one thing that is obvious through the lenses of logic and knowledge is the understanding that when one dies, he/she becomes a *ghost*. Well *ghost* is synonymous to *spirit* and *spirits* are basically made of *light*. However, *ghost* is not synonymous to a *soul*. This logically add to the support of my explanation that *spirit* and *soul* are not the same entity. In some cases, some people mix the meaning and application of these two entities up and get confused with their distinctiveness.

The *spirit* is supernatural because its source is from *The Spirit of spirits*, which is *The Most High*. The *spirit* is not an earthly body. The *spirit* is eternal, it doesn't die like our earthly body does. The *spirit* gravitates naturally towards its source, *The Spirit of spirits*. Resistance by the earthly body to prevent the *spirit* to communicate with *The Spirit of spirits* only leads to spiritual weakness and spiritual death as in malfunctioning (not a physical death). This may also lead to spiritual damnation by *the Spirit of Spirits* who is *The Most High*. The *spirit* is the main way one can communicate with *The Spirit of spirits*. Separating from our earthly body through death is a transition to our full form. Which is *spiritual being*, death is just a transition not the end. Mankind cannot reach their highest form unless they are able to connect with themselves spiritually. The *Holy Spirit of The Most High* is *the Spirit of spirits'* direct impact on/to mankind. It is filled with wisdom, fear with direct respect to reverence of *The Most High*, knowledge, comprehension, fortitude, counsel, and piety. The lack thereof in any of these characteristics indicate that you're distant from *the Spirit of spirits*.

The *soul* is the *consciousness* of this earth. The *soul* is what aids us to live and relate to this material dimension. How one reacts to something or someone such as; to trust, fear, happy, boredom, joy, excitement, terrified, anger, surprises, distaste, fight, flight, and host of actions and emotions to one another is tied to our conscious awareness of the culture we are exposed to. Basically, the characteristics of living things in regard to responding to stimuli, movement, respiration, nutrition, growth, urge to reproduce and to excrete are all linked to the *soul/consciousness*. Everything made from our material world is corruptible including the human body. The *soul* as a memory stores all its encounters on material earth as a recording device right from birth to death. At the time of dying, the *soul* replays all its memories within a moment of

time relative to our material world.

The Most High, The WORD, and The HOLY SPIRIT

The *oneness* of everything in *The Most High* is due to the multiplication factor of *The Most High* (Himself) through *His* creation. This is what I mean by that, everything created by *The Most High* is an extension and expression of *Himself*. Even *His* first instruction to the animals on land and in water including birds, insects, all types of fishes, and unto the first man and woman called Adam was "[be] fruitful and multiply".

The multiplication and replication of one ($1 \times 1 \times 1 \times 1 \times 1 \times 1 \times 1 \times 1 \times 1 \times 1 \times 1 \times 1 = 1$). The woman was created with a rib from the man (Genesis 2:21,22). This means *"oneness"* through multiplication of one. It doesn't matter how many we are on this planet, be it 9 billion or 10 billion; we are all *one* as an entity both in *spiritual* sense and *physical* sense. This apply to all of *The Most High's* creations. It is simple yet complicated for most people to fathom because this is a power manifestation foreign to our physical realm. Reference to Figure 2 and Figure 3 respectively for additional insight.

   The Most High Creator is the *core* of all *His* creations. Since *He* is a *spirit* every communication is executed through spiritual means. The *trinity* concept of *The Most High, His Word* and *His Spirit* (known as the Holy Spirit) is solely *spiritual*. The physical aspect of the *trinity* concept is found in humans as father, mother and child (it's all around us). If you have a child, then you have exhibited the physical manifestation of the *trinity* concept. The Holy Spirit of *The Most High* is in union with *The Most High's* own *Spoken Words* and *The Most High Himself*. I will make sure to break down the *trinity* concept later on with illustrations in this chapter. Do not forget that we are all spirits with our source/origination from *The Most High Creator*. In reference to **Genesis 1:2**, we're introduced to *"the Spirit of God"* which is *The Most High*.

Genesis 1:3 indicates that *"God said...."* which is *The Word of The Most High,* with the *Word* representing *The Most High's "Spoken Word"*. Now in **Genesis 1:6, v9, v11, v14, v20, v24, v26, v28 and v29;** from there you find every *"Spoken Word"* by *The Most High* emphasizing exactly what *The Most High* **said**.

The mystery is beyond human comprehension because it is not contained in our material/physical realm. Let me break down the *trinity* concept a little bit further for you according to the first book of the Torah:

God -------------→ Spoke ----------------→ into Existence.

The Creator.	Means of Creation	*All Creations.*
Spirit of all spirits;	*Spoken Word*	
Holy Spirit.	*Nothing* was *Made* without *The Word*.	
The *Holy Spirit* is	*Word* is of **The Most High.**	
the *Spirit of God.*	*The Word* is **God**; God *Speaks/Spoke*;	
	The Most High's **Word**	

Hence, God is a monotheistic God exemplified in different ways through *His* creations. Never forget that this is a spiritual issue. Hence, using our understanding of things confined to this physical dimension would only cause us more confusion. Something like this requires us to be in the spirit (our true form) in order to understand the nature of God.

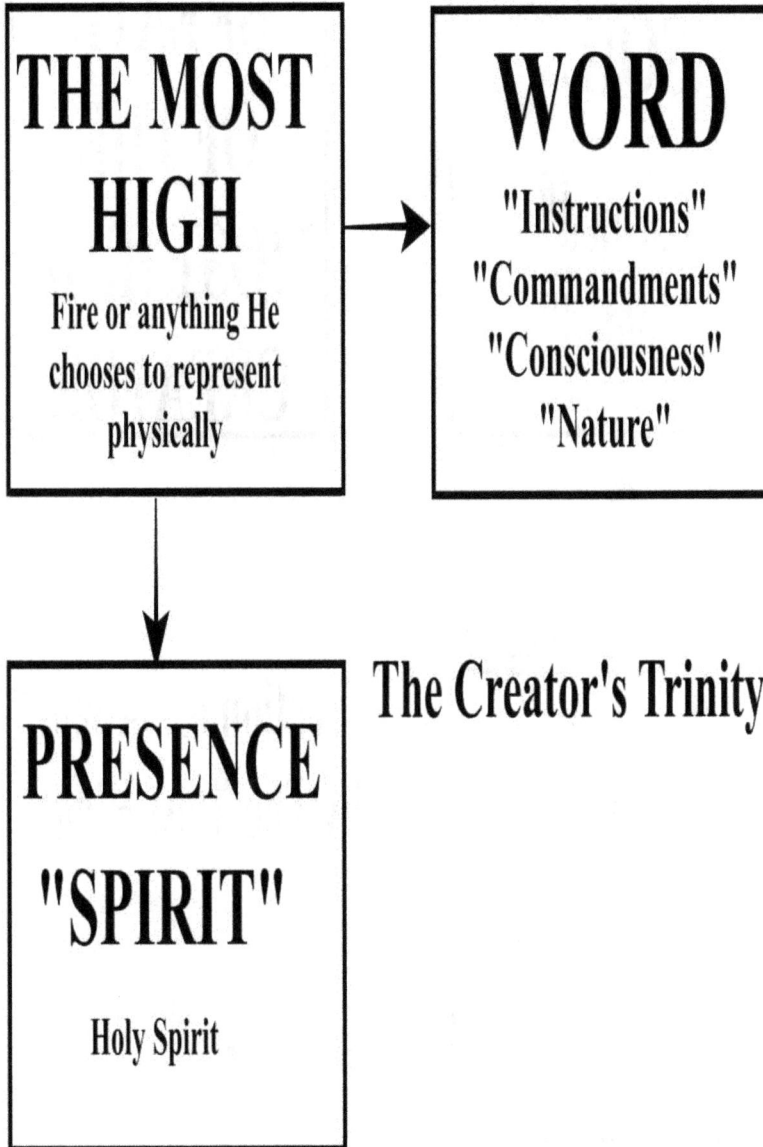

THE MOST HIGH

Fire or anything He chooses to represent physically

WORD

"Instructions"
"Commandments"
"Consciousness"
"Nature"

PRESENCE "SPIRIT"

Holy Spirit

The Creator's Trinity

Fig 12

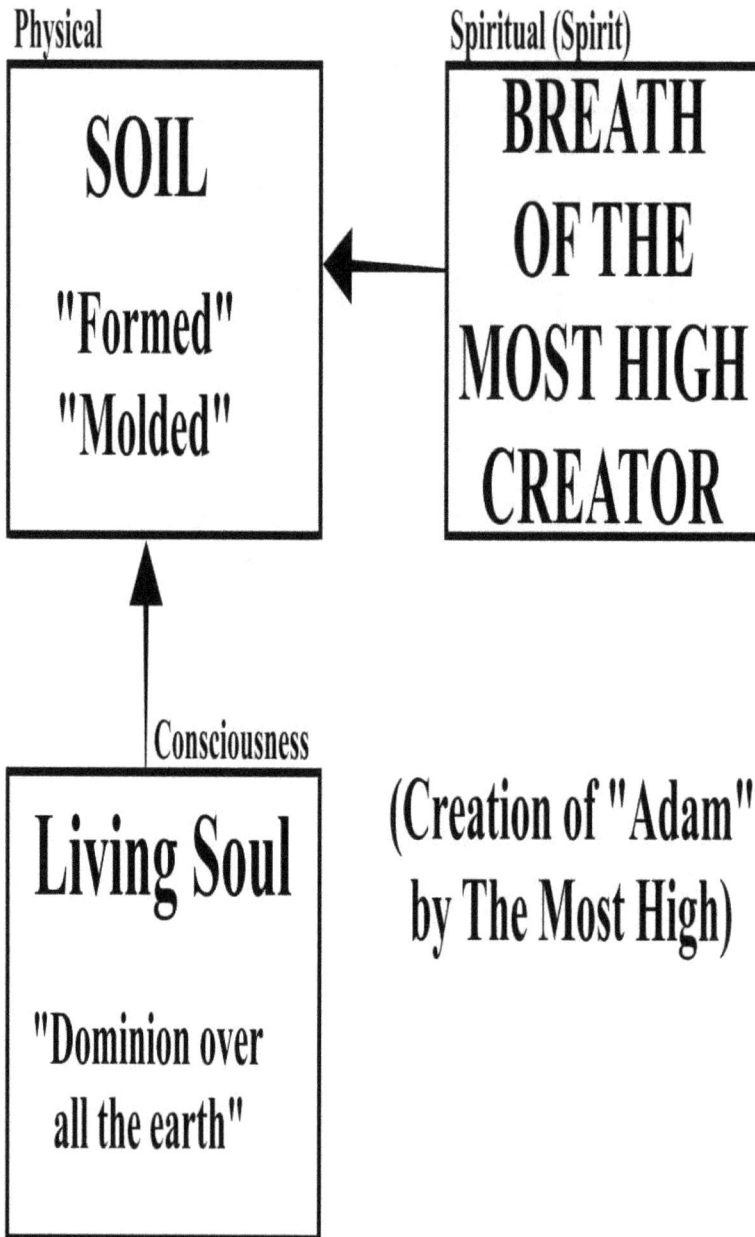

Physical

Spiritual (Spirit)

SOIL

"Formed"
"Molded"

BREATH
OF THE
MOST HIGH
CREATOR

Consciousness

Living Soul

"Dominion over
all the earth"

(Creation of "Adam"
by The Most High)

Fig 13

The Holy Spirit is filled with wisdom, reverence, knowledge, comprehension, fortitude, counsel, and piety. The Holy Spirit is *The Most High's* way of communicating with us through convictions to sanctify our true self (the spirit within us). The easiest way to explain the relationship between the "*God Spirit*" which is the Holy Spirit and the spirit in humans is to liken it to that of a magnet. They both attract each other. The human spirit is recharged, refilled, re-energized, and sanctified when linked to the Holy Spirit.

What stands in the way between the Holy Spirit and the human spirit is the *"right use"* or the *"misuse"* of our *Free Will*. If you feel disconnected from *The Most High's* spirit, then it is because you are choosing to use your *Free Will* as a means to move away from *The Most High*. Remember, *The Most High* is love and *He* is Omnipresent. You just have to consciously use your *Free Will* to <u>choose</u> to be in communication with *Him*. *The Most High* gave you that choice and you ought to use it wisely.

According to Christianity and Catholics, the *Son of God* is, the *Word* of God or God's *Spoken Word* meaning *logos*. This is not something I ascribe to because I do not personally accept or follow the *"New Testament"* books because its writers are very questionable. Some people even attest the *New Testament* authorship to the Piso Family whereby one of them authored under the name of Flavius Josephus (at your discretion, you can read about *"The Complete Works of Flavius Josephus"* translated by William Whiston). Also, there are lot of questionable irregularities in the so called "gospels" of the *New Testaments* with respect to Mary and Joseph's lineages. I will tackle some of the numerous irregularities later on in this chapter to expose such a fictional writing as the *New Testament* books. You are always welcome to research on the names and references stated above to expand your knowledge on the authorship of the *New Testament* books. For fair assessment of this topic, let's look at the following

New Testament bible verses that claim to make a case for

Iesus, as the *Word*:

<u>*John 1:1 – 3 KJV*</u>

*In the beginning was **the Word**, and **the Word** was with God, and **the Word** was God.*

*[2] **The same** was in the beginning with God.*

*[3] **All things** were **made by him**; and **without him** was **not any thing made that was made**.*

Also;

<u>*Hebrews 1:1 – 3,5,7 KJV*</u>

*God, who at sundry times and in divers manners **spake** in time past unto the fathers by the prophets,*

*[2] Hath in these last days **spoken** unto us **by his Son**, whom he **hath appointed heir of all things**, by whom also **he made the worlds;***

*[3] Who being the brightness of his glory, and the express image of his person, and upholding all things by **the word** of his power, when he had by himself purged our sins, **sat down on the right hand of the Majesty on high**:*

*[5] For unto which of the angels said he at any time, **Thou art my Son**, this day have I begotten thee? **And again, I will be to him a Father, and he shall be to me a Son?***

*[7] And of the **angels** he saith, Who maketh his angels spirits, and his ministers **a flame of fire**.*

Per the *New Testament* readings above, Iesus is the head of all God's creations known and unknown to mankind. Iesus is the image, a physical representation of the *Godhead;* also, a *Spirit* with a physical manifestation and representation of God. All dominions, powers, judgement, creations and literally everything is crowned to Iesus and it is through Iesus that every creation came into existence since Iesus is *The Word* per the *New Testament*. Hence, Christians and Catholics hold that; Iesus is the **creator** of all things since he is represented as *The Word*. Look at the verse below, this is another view from the Christians:

Colossians 1:12 – 20 KJV

*[12] Giving thanks unto **the Father**, which hath made us meet to be partakers of the inheritance of the saints in light:*

*[13] Who hath delivered us from the power of darkness, **and hath translated us into the kingdom of his dear Son:***

[14] In whom we have redemption through his blood, even the forgiveness of sins:

*[15] **Who is the image of the invisible God, the firstborn of every creature:***

*[16] **For by him were all things created**, that are in heaven, and that are in earth, visible and invisible, whether they be thrones, or dominions,*

or principalities, or powers: all things were created by him, and for him:

[17] And he is before all things, and by him all things consist.

[18] And he is the head of the body, the church: who is the beginning, the firstborn from the dead; that in all things he might have the preeminence.

*[19] **For it pleased the Father that in him should all fulness dwell;***

*[20] And, **having made peace through the blood of his cross, by him to reconcile all things unto himself; by him, I say, whether they be things in earth, or things in heaven.***

There is only one *Most High Creator* and nothing else. *The Most High's* Omnipotence, Omnipresence and Omniscience is far beyond human comprehension. *The Most High* does not cause confusion but peace, clarity, purity and understanding. Whenever you feel conflicted about God and His magnificent splendor, I encourage you to pray (communicate with *The Most High*) for understanding and *He* will show you the way.

I am going to now explain the *trinity* concept: *The Most High*, *The Most High's **Word*** and the **Holy Spirit** of *The Most High* with illustrations for those that are visual learners. Let's have a look at the following:

Fig.14 Christians/Catholics/New Testament view

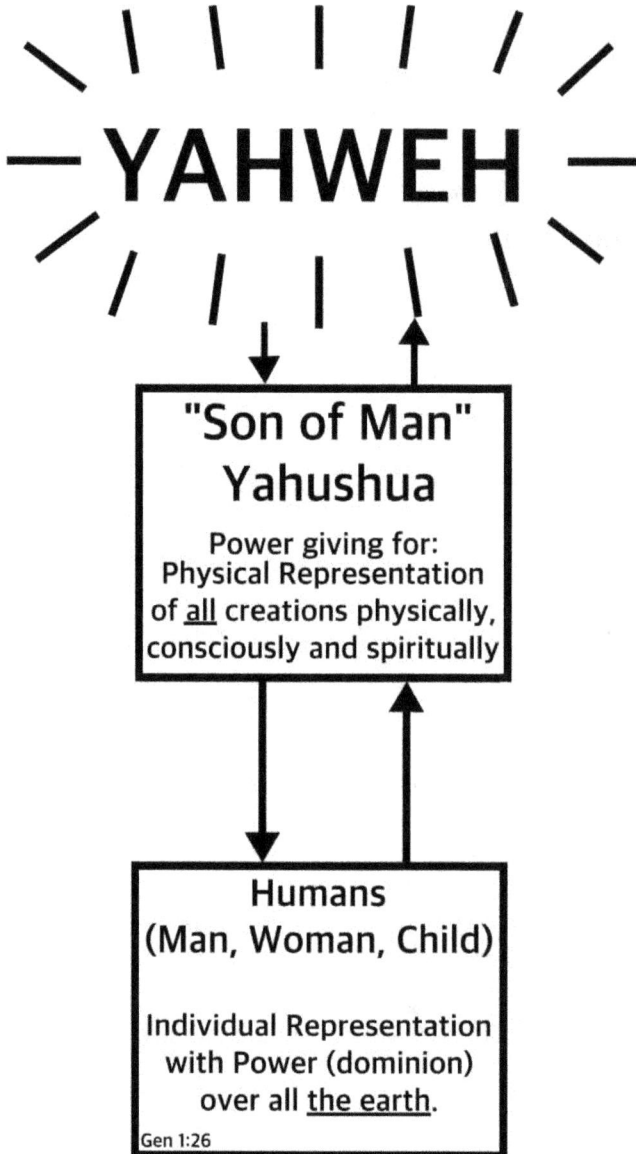

YAHWEH

"Son of Man" Yahushua

Power giving for:
Physical Representation
of all creations physically,
consciously and spiritually

Humans
(Man, Woman, Child)

Individual Representation
with Power (dominion)
over all the earth.

Gen 1:26

The Father (Love is His core) His character/ integrity/role

His Son (Image/ flesh) Physical Representation of God
Interacts with all creations within the physical domain

God

His Spirit (Holy Spirit) - Spirit of God

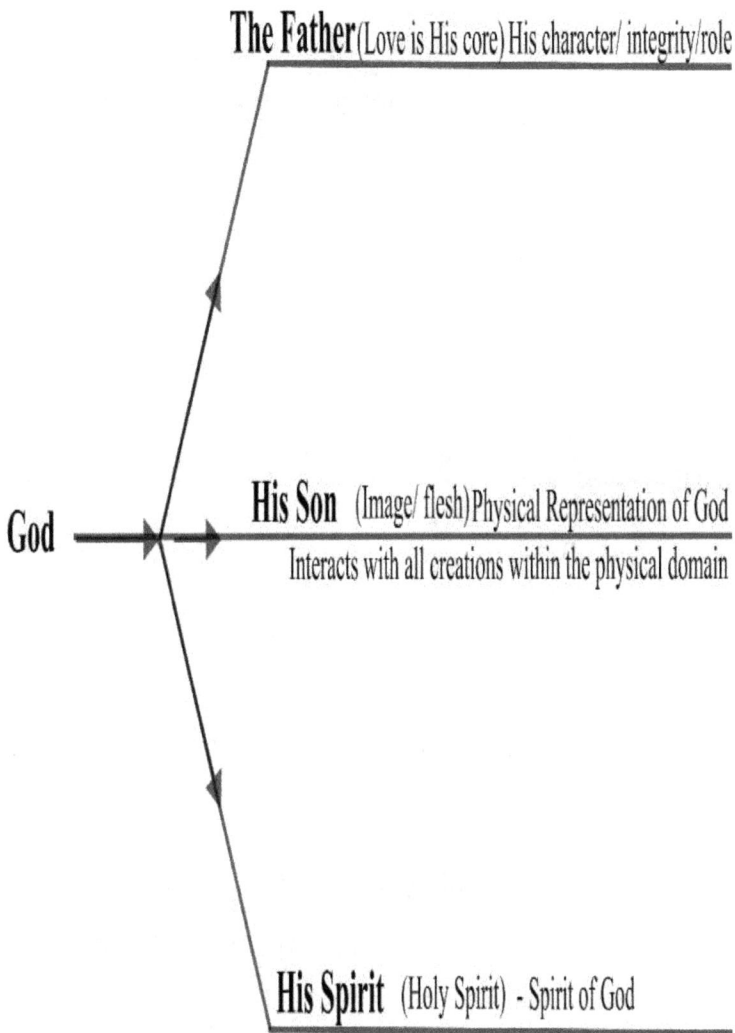

Fig.15 **Christians/Catholics/New Testament view**

Flesh (Physical package)

↑ Earthly cloth to interact within our physical realm

activates

Soul (Consciousness/ awareness)

↑

activates

Spirit (Core is Love) [Lives forever]

Its origination is God (The Spirit of all Spirits)

Human ───→

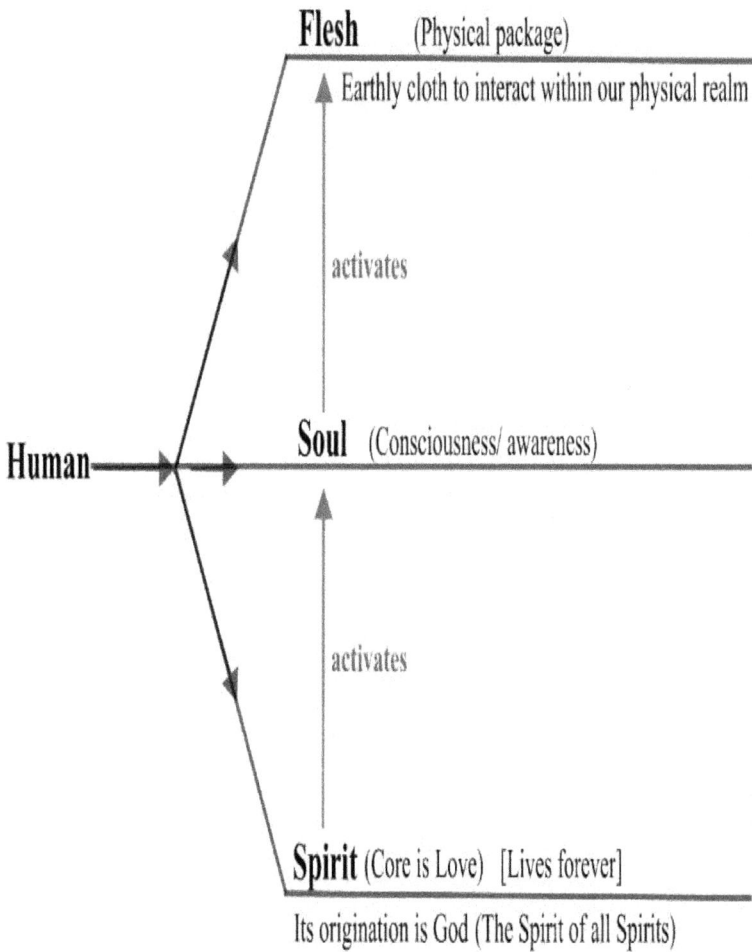

Fig.16 This illustration (Fig.14) depicts the flow of mankind's

creation, Adam (male and female) by *The Most High* according to

Genesis, the first book of the Torah. The *Torah* are a collection of the

first five (5) books of the Old Testament. Torah means "instructions" or

"law".

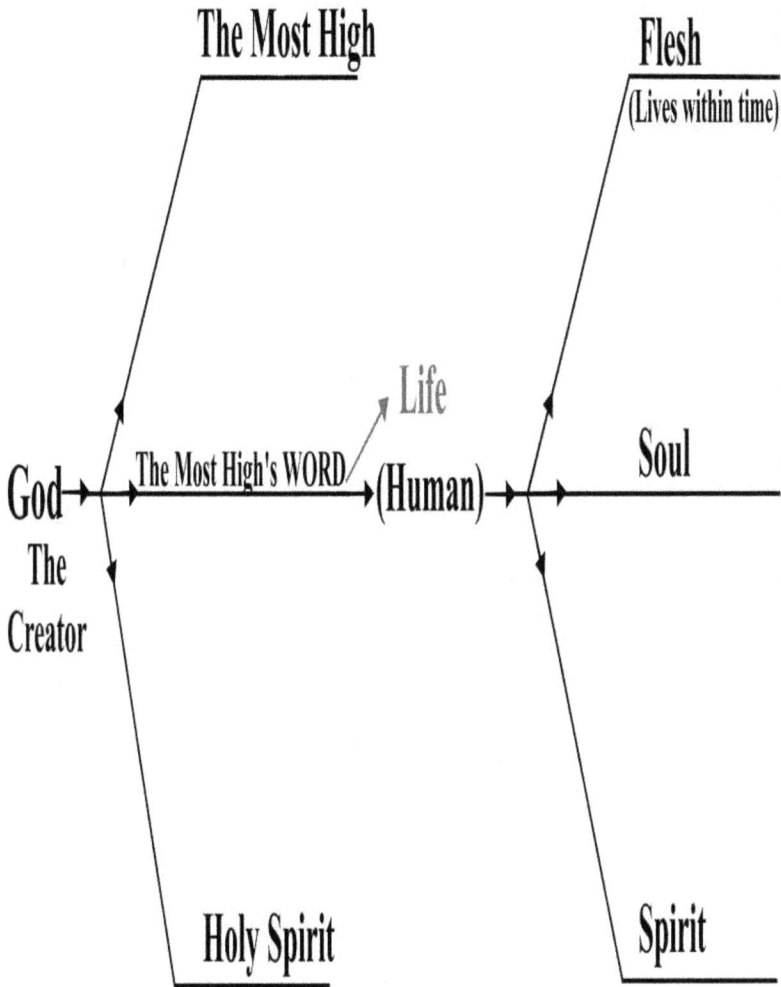

Fig.17 Combination of the Torah's account on Adam's creation together with *The Most High's Own **Word*** and *His Spirit.* I ascribe to the *Torah* and the *"Old Testament"* books (Tanakh).

Illustration (Fig.18) below unfolds what happens to us after ***physical death*** (when the flesh seizes to exist, no more consciousness – the soul departs) what lives forever is the human *spirit*; it gravitates towards its *origination* for a *decision* on where it spends eternity to be made by *The Most High, The Creator* of All Things. The human *spirit* will await a **decision** (*Time* is irrelevant/holds no substance in the spiritual domain).

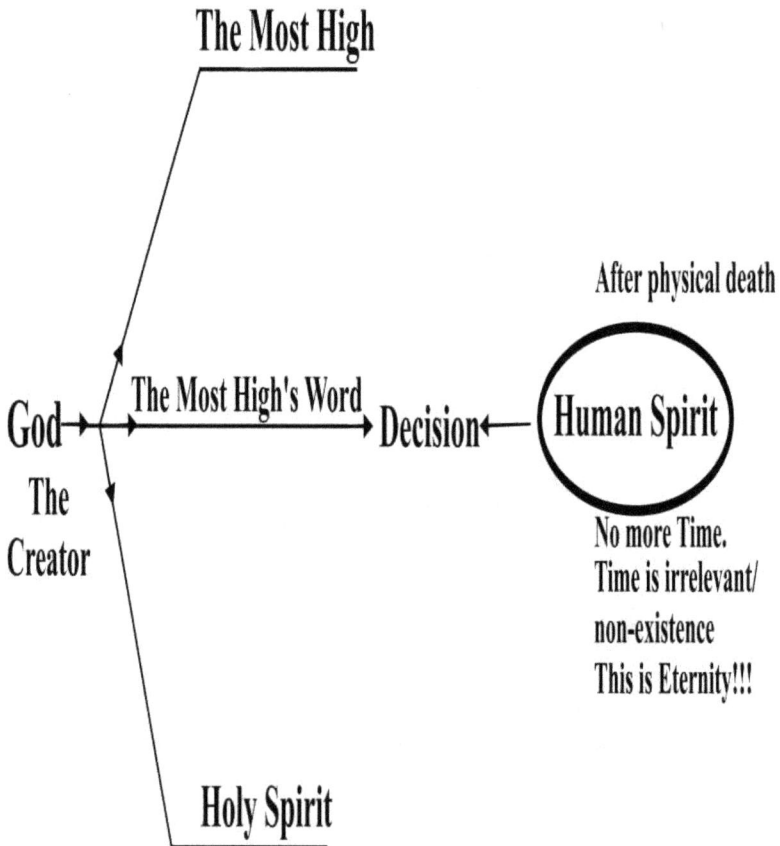

The Most High

After physical death

God → The Most High's Word → Decision ← Human Spirit

The Creator

Holy Spirit

No more Time.
Time is irrelevant/
non-existence
This is Eternity!!!

Fig.18

THE TRINITY EXPRESSED IN HUMANITY

The *trinity* in humanity is compactly intertwined within the aura of humanity in the *trinity* of *The Most High*. **The Father, Mother and Child** are one as a "whole" in spirit, consciousness and flesh. The oneness of this unique existence remains unchanged regardless of its multiplicity. The diagrammatic explanations below add additional emphasis to *"The Trinity Expressed in Humanity"*.

Fig.19

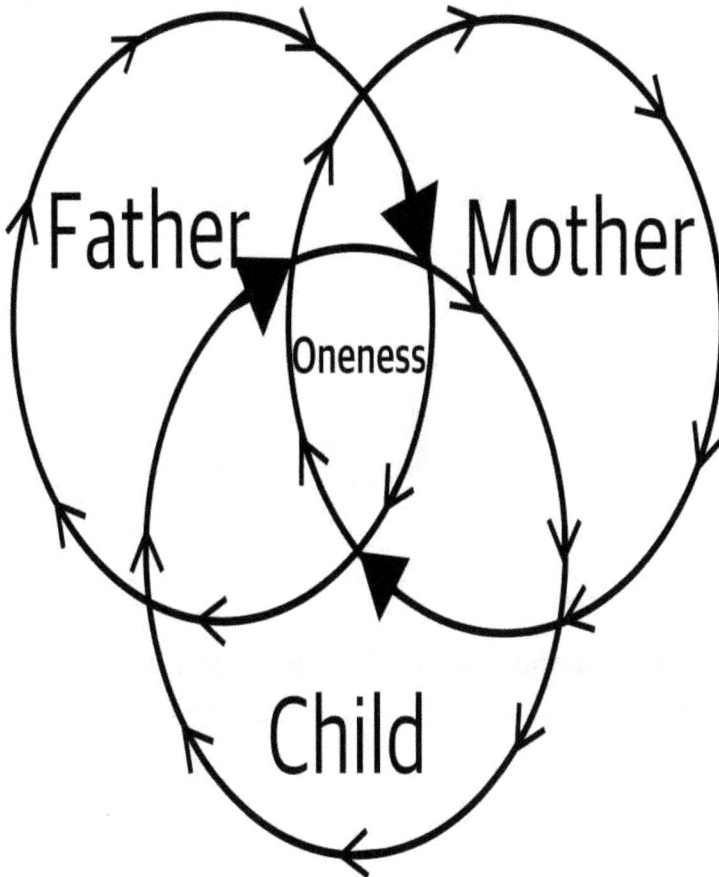

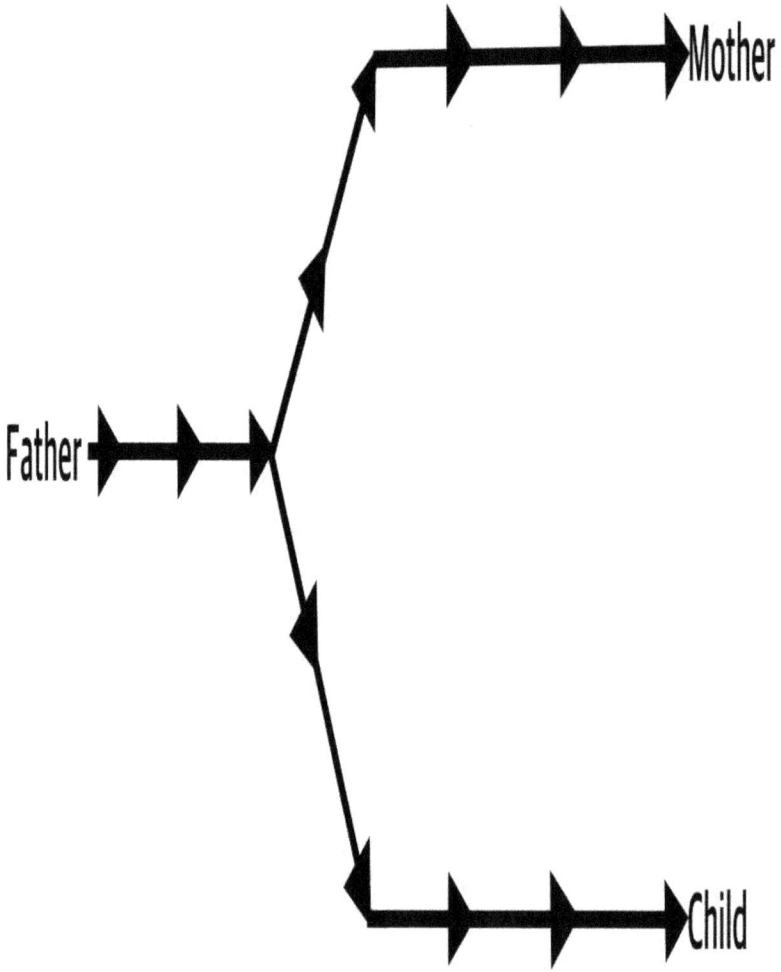

Fig. 20

The Father, Mother, and Child form *the trinity in humanity* is manifested physically and spiritually.

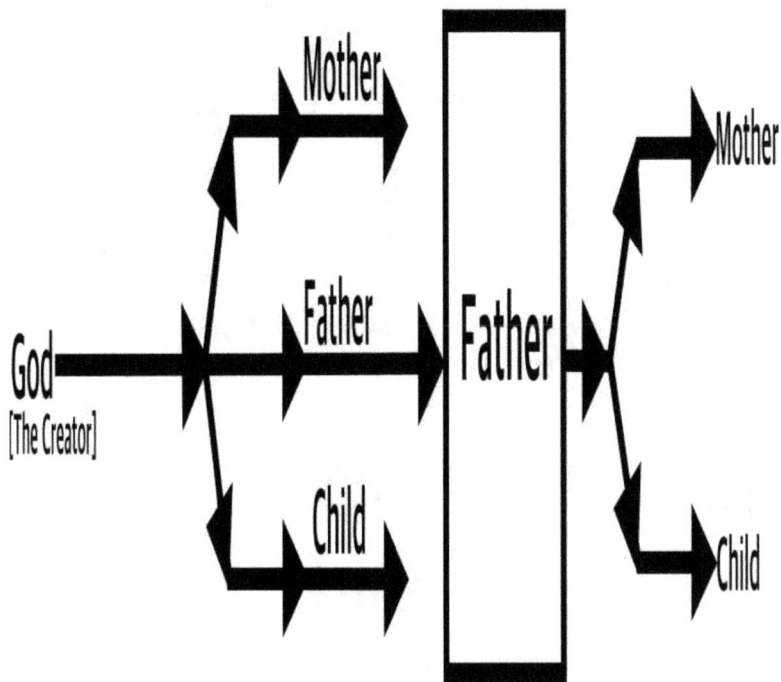

Fig.21

Everything originates from *The Most High Creator* and is manifested through projected multiplicity through the lens of predestination that has been ordained and orchestrated within time's conception. *The trinity expressed in humanity* is a daily reminder of the greatness and undeniable providence of the *Creator, The Most High*.

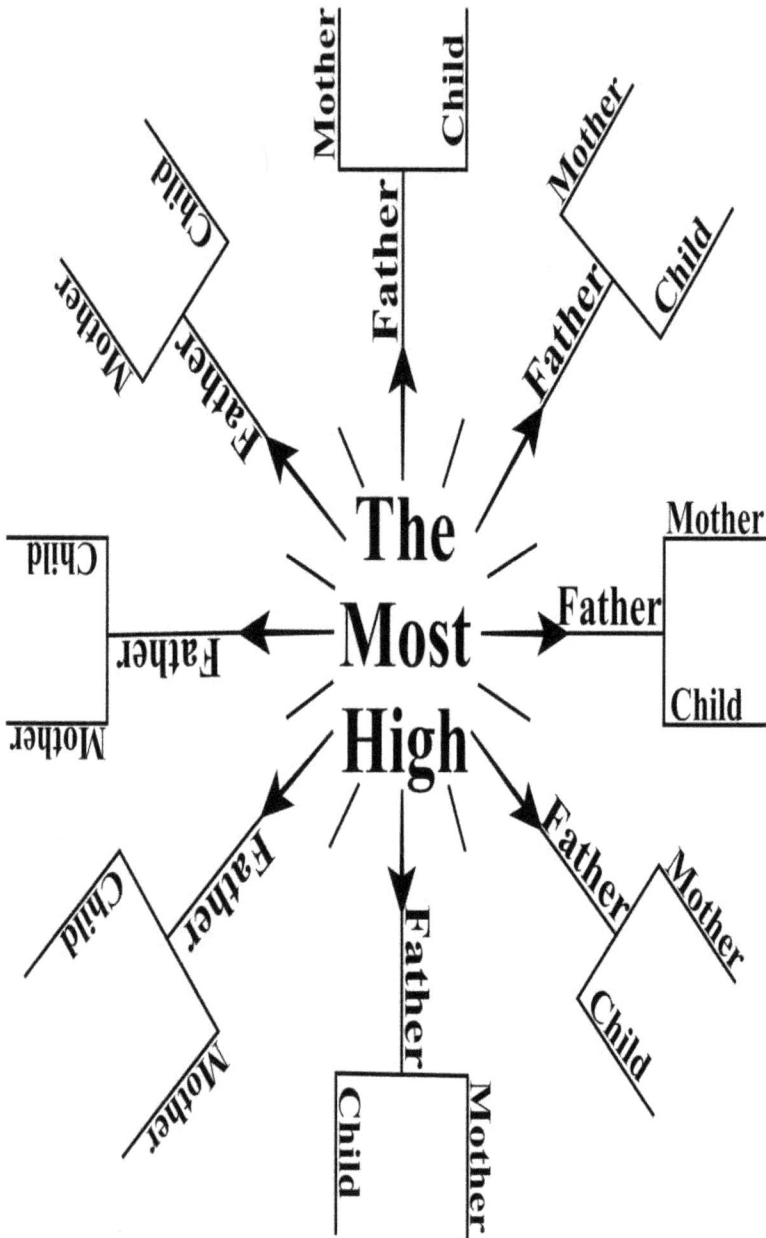

Fig 22

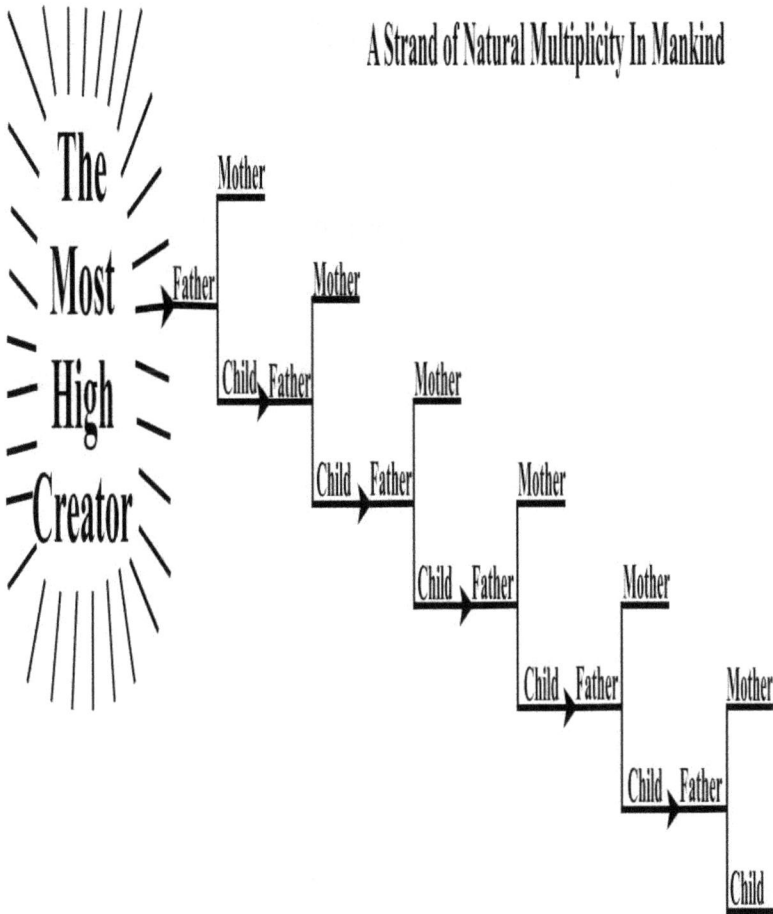

Fig 23

The *Father*, the *Mother* and the *Child* make up the *trinity* exemplified by *The Most High Creator* through *His* creation of Adam (male and female); (man and woman).

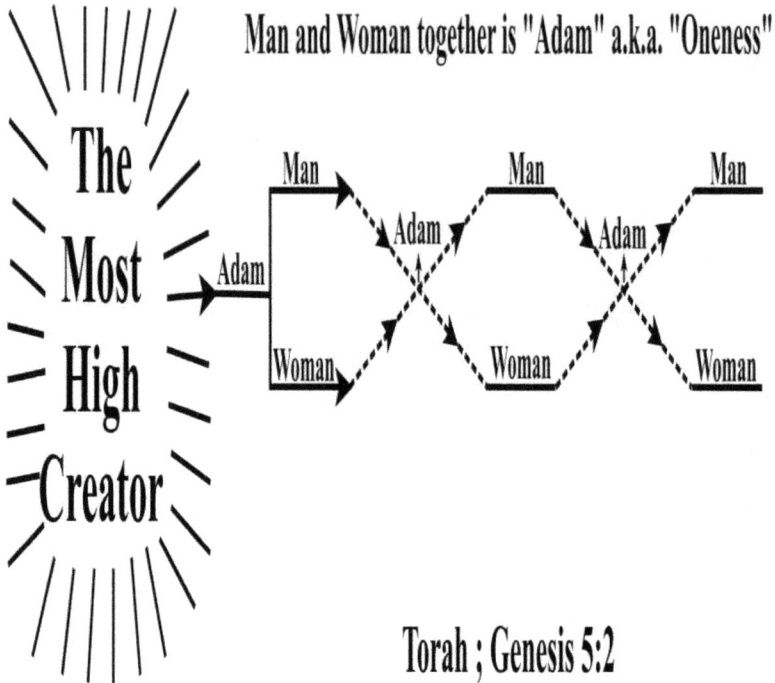

Man and Woman together is "Adam" a.k.a. "Oneness"

Torah ; Genesis 5:2

Fig 24 Original multiplicity of originality in <u>*Oneness.*</u>

From the first book of the *Torah,* **Genesis 5:2** *The Most High* called both the male and female (man and woman) as **Adam**. Adam is <u>*Oneness*</u> of the male and female creation. Read the verse below:

Genesis 5:2 *"**Male** and **female** created he **them**; and blessed **them**, and called <u>**their name Adam**</u>, in the day when they were created."*

Know for a fact that it was the male (man) who named the female as "*Eve*". Read this in *Genesis 3:20*.

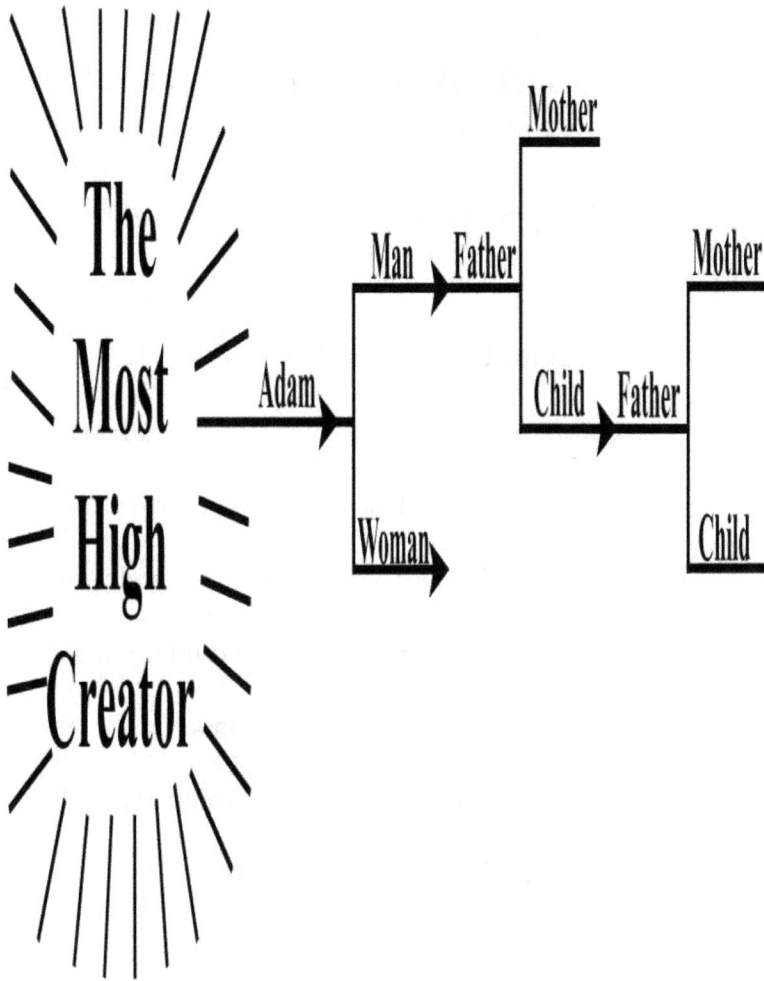

Fig 25

We can be a trillion in the world populace, but we are all an origination of "*One Original*" multiplicity.

THE TORAH'S RECORD OF LINEAGE TRUMPS THE NEW TESTAMENT AS A FICTIONAL BOOK

The *Torah* consists of five books that are deemed the instructions, laws, culture, traditions and teachings of the original people of the bible. From the *Torah*, we know that the chosen tribe is *Jacob a.k.a Israel* (12 tribes of Israel). This is so because mankind departed from the *ways* and *instructions* of *The Most High* to make smaller gods out of sand, wood and clay. These smaller gods could not talk, eat, move, or see. Mankind became evil (opposite from peace, love and unity with one another) through war, paganism, unethical breeding and destruction.

Now, *the traditions*, *cultures* and *instructions* of *The Most High* per the *Torah* with direct respect to the lineages was through the *father's line*. Therefore, since the time of Adam; records indicate the flow of this line of lineage to be sovereign and ordained by *The Most High*.

125

However, the *New Testament* bible of the Christians and

Catholics has massive irregularities of this very *instruction*

from *The Most High*. I will outline these irregularities with

illustrations, direct verses from the same *New Testament*

bible and explanation on how obvious the irregularities are

shown. This is one of the major reasons why I do not

ascribe to the *New Testament* bible of the Christians and

Catholics. I see the *New Testament* accounts to be fictional

and plagiarized from the **Torah** and the rest of the **Old**

Testament books.

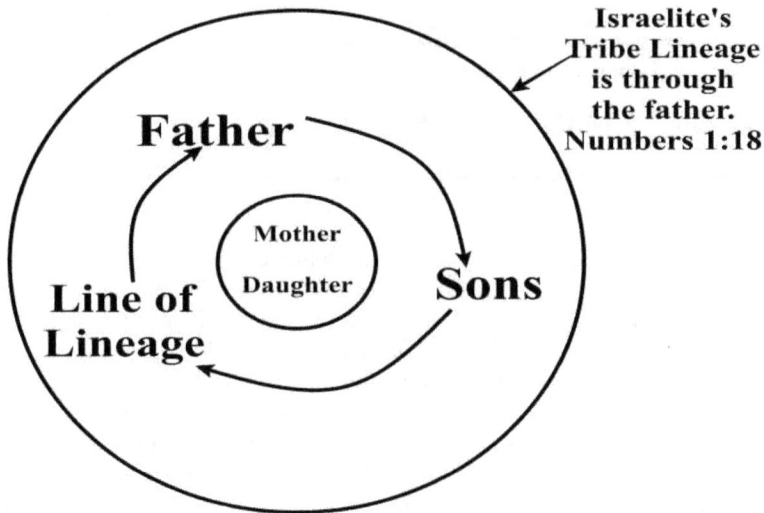

fig.26

```
┌─────────────────┐
│  SON OF MAN     │ ━━━━━▶  Born of Man & Woman
└─────────────────┘
        │
┌─────────────────┐
│ DAUGHTERS OF MAN│ ━━━━━▶  Born of Man & Woman
└─────────────────┘
        │
┌─────────────────┐
│ISRAEL TRADITIONS│ ━━━━━▶  Through Father's Lineage
│    LINEAGE      │
└─────────────────┘
        │
┌─────────────────┐
│   PRE-FLOOD     │ ━━━━━▶  Through Father's Lineage
│    LINEAGE      │
└─────────────────┘
        │
┌─────────────────┐
│   POST-FLOOD    │ ━━━━━▶  Through Father's Lineage
│    LINEAGE      │
└─────────────────┘
        │
┌──────────────────────────┐
│   CONSISTENCY IS KEY      │
│ GOD THE CREATOR IS NOT A GOD │
│       OF CONFUSION        │
└──────────────────────────┘
        │
┌──────────────────────────┐
│ A SON OF MAN IS A SON OF MAN │
└──────────────────────────┘
```

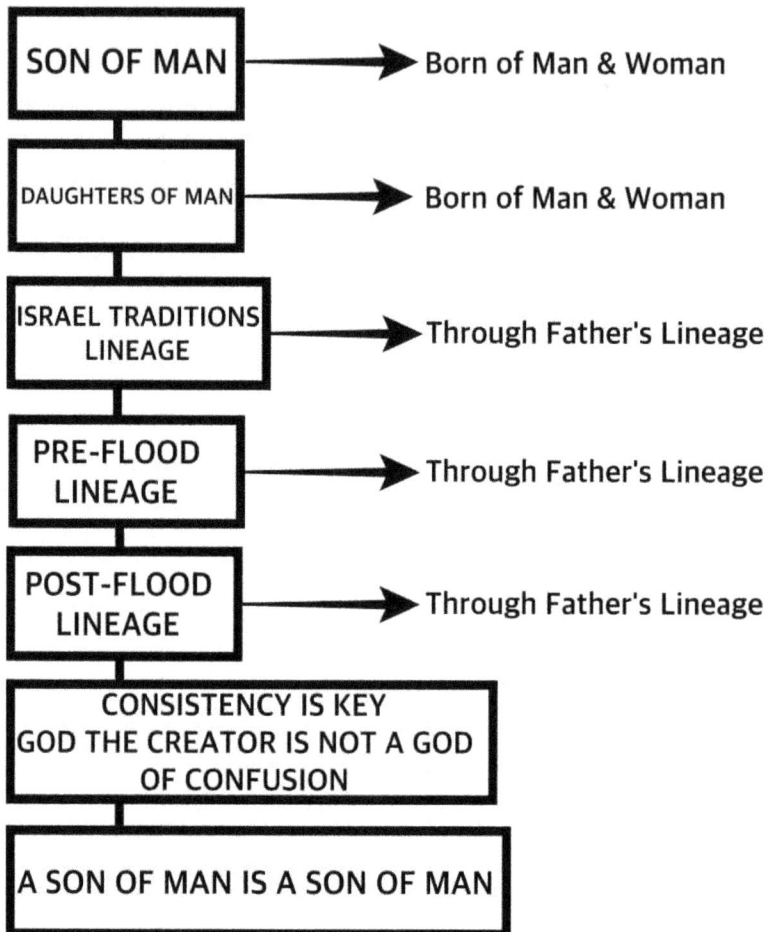

Fig. 27 NOTE: <u>Sons of man</u> are not the same as <u>Sons of Elohiym</u> (Son of God). In Hebrew and Aramaic *Sons of Elohiym* refer to supernatural beings or angels while *Sons of man* refers to mankind ("of man and woman", "flesh and blood", frail and weak). When *The Most High* indicated through the prophets about the *Son of Man* coming from the *Tribe of Judah /house of David* to save the nation of Israel (all the 12 tribes). *The Most High* was very specific, clear and wasn't confused (Confusion is not of *The Most High*). Read these versus: ***Gen.6:2,4; Job1:6;2:1; Job38:7; Daniel 3:25; Gen 4:25(Seth=Son of Man; flesh)*** The <u>*Son of Man*</u> is born of a <u>man and woman</u> <u>chosen</u> by YHWH.

Numbers 1:18 → Should always be from father's lineage

oldest of all 4 gospels ↑

Mark & John "No infancy record of Iesus" nothing No genealogy

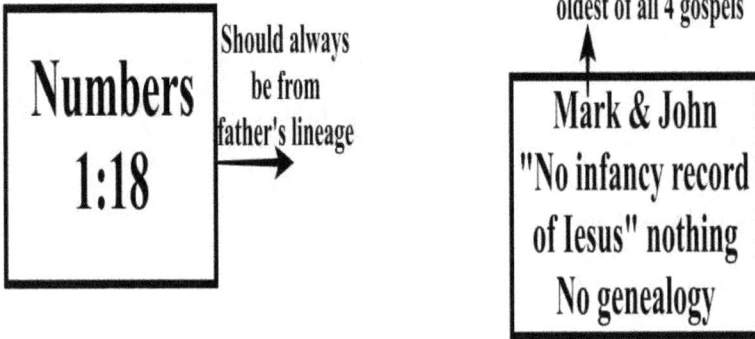

Mary (Iesus mom) is NOT from the tribe of JUDAH/ David

Mary's genealogy NOT in New Testament

ONLY Joseph's genealogy outlined in both Matthew 1 & Luke 3 New Testament

Luke 1:27 Joseph is from Tribe of Judah

Joseph is **NOT** Iesus' biological **father**

Fig. 28

Luke states

Mary

Luke 2:4 (Joseph is from lineage of David)
NOT Mary

cousin of

Elizabeth
Luke 1:36

Descendant
of
Aaron

High Priest

Levi
Tribe

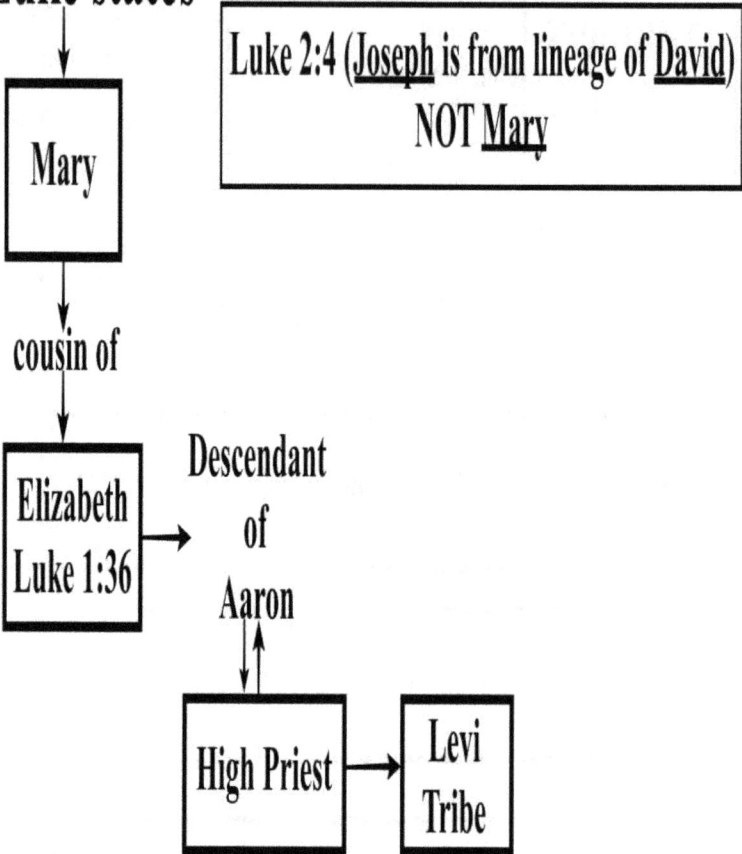

NO Physical LINK between DAVID's SEED and Iesus

Fig. 29

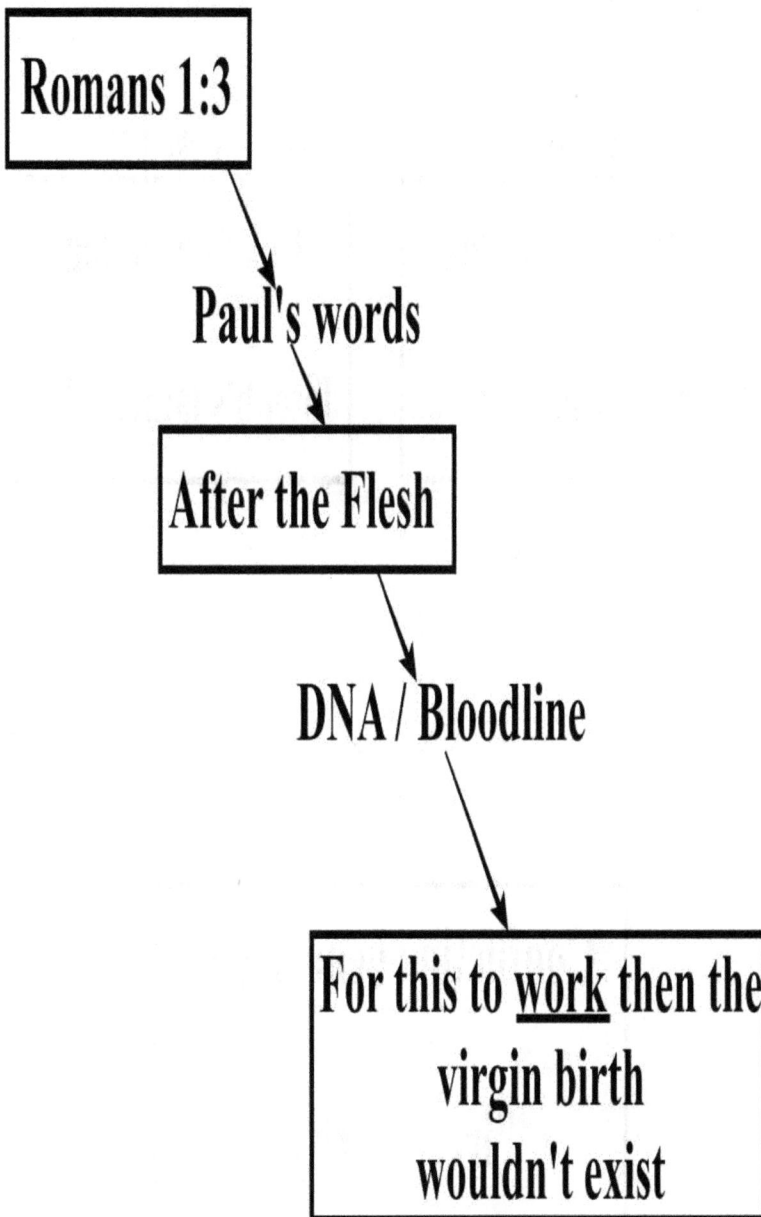

Romans 1:3

Paul's words

After the Flesh

DNA / Bloodline

For this to <u>work</u> then the virgin birth wouldn't exist

Fig. 30

Fig. 31

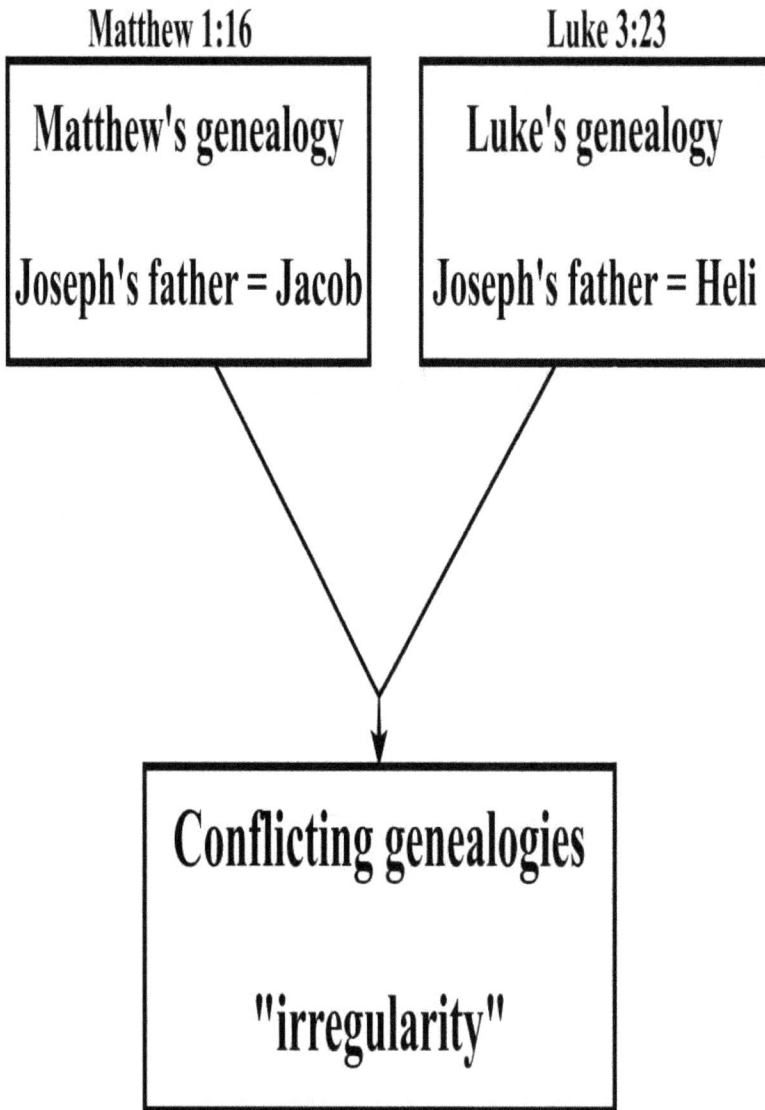

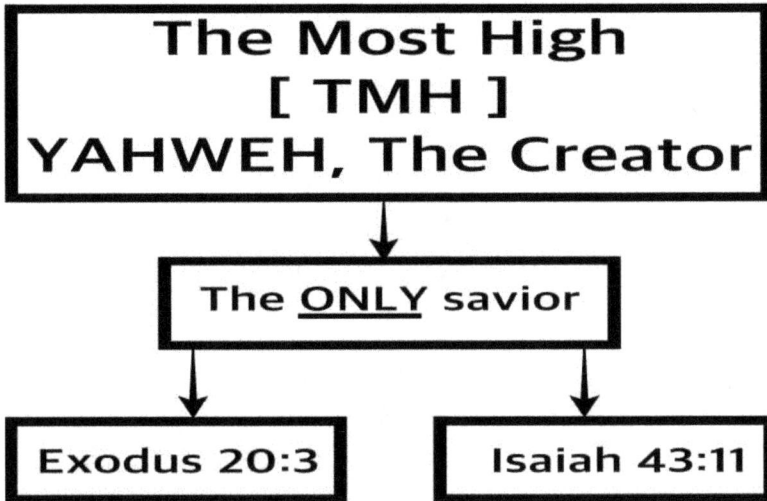

Fig.32

Figure 26 above clearly states the commandment and words of *The Most High* commanding and instructing that there is **no other savior apart from Himself**. This again exposes the Christians and Catholics' New Testament bible to be false, fictional, and contrary to *The Most High*. I choose to be on the side of *The Most High Creator* than to follow the crowd of lies and irregularities contained in the New Testament bible that was basically forced on people through colonization and slavery. Even there is a *"slave bible"* that was strictly forced on slaves to remain in slavery. Below are the versus that *The Most High Creator* clearly **stated** and **commanded** that <u>there is no other savior apart from himself.</u>

Exodus 20:3

*"Thou shalt have **no other gods** <u>before me</u>." -by The Most High*

Isaiah 43:11

*"I, even I, am <u>the YAHUAH</u>; and **beside me there is <u>no</u> savior**."*

132

CHAPTER 7

CHAPTER 7

SCIENTIFICAL, BIBLICAL, GEOGRAPHICAL, AND ARCHAEOLOGICAL EVIDENCE.

Section 1

The thought, evidence, study and analysis of *The Most High's* existence is the biggest topic on the planet. The thought of *The Most High's* existence alone tends to be too great for our human mind to comprehend let alone to decipher it to the core. Before I tap into the scientific, geographical, biblical and archaeological evidences of *The Most High*; I would want you to think about the word *faith*. What is *faith*? Do you have *faith* in yourself? Do you have *faith* in life? Do you have *faith* in your partner, fiancée, wife, family, children, or the universe? Some of us are too quick to counter when it comes to the word *faith* because some of us link the word *faith* to a religion, doctrine, or

ideological means. We all live and execute our daily

responsibilities based on *faith*. Everyday *faith* is the

foundation of your *"why"* you do what you do even without

knowing the outcome in most cases. A simple example is

when you wake up in the morning, although you do not

know how the day will end; you somehow have plans for

the day due to a routine or schedule.

Let me expand on the example given above, regardless

of how tight or flexible your daily plans may be; you still

have no control over how things will turn out throughout

the day or at the end of the day. However, you get up from

bed, prepare and attend to your day's activities with **faith**.

Believing through the execution of your actions or works

(responsibilities) that everything is going to go as planned.

Taking risk is an art of giving *faith* a chance to function in

your life. Faith is the backbone of our daily movements.

Our faith in something, someone or oneself precipitate

confidence, conviction, discipline, leadership, success and trust. Now, let's get back to the scientific, geographical, biblical and archaeological evidences of *The Most High.*

Epistemologically, mankind is able to gain knowledge via justification, questioning between reason, belief and opinion. I will go out boldly to say that **knowledge** in all aspects (acquired via science, law, philosophy, medicine, astronomy, archaeology et al) is limited whereas **wisdom** is limitless (no restrictions). *Knowledge* is awarded a degree, a standard, a discipline, a focus which is controlled by men and women with power and influence. Through wars, colonization and bullying, one's *knowledge* about somethings could easily be manipulated. The flaw in *knowledge* is the art of its truths and facts being hidden, kept as a secret or has not yet been uncovered. Hence, relying on *knowledge* alone may intellectually and spiritually cripple you from ever tapping into your *"supernatural self"*.

On the other hand, *wisdom's* characteristic nature solely originates from *The Most High. Wisdom* is *The Most High's* footstool; it is neither corrupt nor prideful. Carnal man/woman can never taste a glimpse of such *wisdom*. This is where *faith* in *The Most High* comes in just in case you were wondering. However, majority of mankind are deep asleep. They seek and desire things from the wrong source instead of redirecting their hearts, minds, thoughts and being towards the everlasting fountain of *wisdom* that only *The Most High* possesses.

With that in mind, let us dig into our spiritual self of comprehension and use the evidence of our planet and galaxies to help us get closer to embracing *The Most High's* existence. Since the time of Adam, mankind has struggled and toiled to find their way back to *The Most High*. Archaeologists have done terrific job to unveil some of the evidence that support *The Most High's* existence and interactions with mankind. Archaeological findings which constitute landscapes, arts, artifacts, architecture, bio, eco, non-bio and non-eco facts support historical civilizations, stories, writings, beliefs and movements. Science with its branches, physical science (astronomy, physics, chemistry and geology) mathematics and logic (abstract concepts with formula) and social science (as the name implies: society and mankind's direct or indirect relationship to it) was derived from our world, environment or universe to collect data, research, and analysis to theorized and attempt to prove the existence of *The Most High* (the true *Creator* of everything). We will also look into the biblical approach on this subject matter to have a holistic view about *The Most High* – the *creator* and *ruler* of everything.

I want to quickly state that, I love science but in my candid understanding, science is just a way for us to understand our world and the numerous worlds around us. What we think we know right now in science is one-zillionth of what is out there in and outside our world.

Science is good, science should strongly be pursued but science can never prove the existence of *The Most High* because *The Most High* is far bigger and greater than anything scientists can ever imagine or detect with their instruments, formula or strategies. It is my hope that science will bring people closer to embracing the true *Most High Creator* and for everyone to accept the greatness, magnificence and limitless power of *Him*. There are zillions upon zillions of stars, dimensions, galaxies, particles, substances, earthly and heavenly bodies that are currently unknown to astronomers, various branches of science and mankind. The complexity of our world with its oceans and its inhabitants, the lands, lost civilizations, unanswered geological and geographical discoveries and the ones yet to be discovered even right here on earth are far beyond our reach of comprehension. The amazing thing is that, we have numerous resources, documents and evidence of things found all pointing to the existence of a true intelligent creator.

Scientifically, biblically and Archaeologically there are lots of evidences about God's existence. Instead of giving you the reader the easy way out by breaking down these evidences, I will rather summarize them and list some of the numerous studies, findings and resources to support the evidence of *The Most High's* existence. Nonetheless, this will require you to go on a "scavenger" hunt to research and dig out these information for your intellectual, spiritual, moral, and evidential growth. You will need to put in some personal work. You will need to research some of the lists. This way, you will gain satisfaction. Your questions about this topic would be answered and lastly, you will be honest with yourself about your findings, its meaning and interpretations. **Section II**, will underline some of the scientific, biblical and archaeological ways mankind has been trying to discover *The Most High*, the true *creator* of the universe, and evidence of proof of *The Most High's* existence from the bible as well as archaeological support of the findings that only lead to proofs of the one true *Most High's* existence.

Mankind will never be *The Most High* despite their hard attempts through all levels of science and numerous explorations to get closer to *The Most High's* level. This will never happen; it will rather lead to the destruction of mankind. There is nothing wrong with inventions because our *Creator* is an inventor. *The Most High* created you and everything in the universe hence you possess the gifts to invent things. Ethically, everything is wrong with science's attempt to invent or create another human in our own image. This is extreme and a path that will only lead to damnation. Genetic mutations, machine/tube babies, artificial intelligence with human memories or consciousness, vaccinations to cause sterilization in people around the world. Stealing resources around the world by using fear through threat of bombings and war. Slaughtering each other, a reason of thought here; the ones with the nukes and guns are not the strongest in the world. They just have the advantage - that's it; in that, any third world country or military can become superpower with nuclear weapons (nukes), sophisticated bombs and military accoutrements. What makes one strong is one's spiritual stamina. Every physical thing is temporary but spiritual things are eternal.

The reason of thought was not to go off tangent but to emphasize an important example of how mankind deceives themselves as smart, peaceful, loving and caring. In all actuality, it has been about greed, killing others to rule, thirst for power and selfishness. Mankind has lost its true purpose and now we are in a barbaric era with evil things covered up and controlled by those with influence and power. Middle East was originally part of Africa (including Israel), 99 percent of current Europe was called Rome.

Rome was just divided into ten and three of the ten regions was annihilated from existence. The seven regions left later on became the Europe we know today. If you pause reading right now to research, you will easily find some of these facts with ease. Geographically, nations and regions were just renamed by those who win wars, but the true history remain intact to date. *The Most High* knows *His* own.

Well, now let's proceed with some digging of facts and intellectual fun about somethings that some of us might have read about. Such as, the *Fallen Angels* or known by some as the *Annunaki;* they genetically manipulated through engineering of the human dna as well as plants and other animal cells. It is well known that, the *Annunaki* or *Fallen Angels* had biological kids with women on earth, mixed with trees, birds, sea creatures, and various kinds of animals. They were technologically advanced and civilized than our current civilization. Then, the flood happened

(Read the Book of Enoch, the Sumerian tablets, the book of Genesis with Noah for details).

Section II

ARCHAEOLOGICAL and GEOGRAPHICAL FINDINGS IN RELATION TO THE LOGIC OF THE MOST HIGH'S EXISTENCE.

Archaeological and geographical studies have done tremendous work in digging out human's history from geological and geographical sites to reveal the facts about mankind's existence in times past. It all leads to the proof of discovery of some of the most sophisticated technological, cultural and traditional civilizations bigger and greater than our current time. The amazement of the findings relates to pre-historic flood on earth revealing that the bible has connections and truths to these archaeological findings. As I stated in **section 1**, I encourage my readers to do personal research of their own in addition to the revelations of these archaeological and geographical facts. I encourage you to use this book as a resource. The greater part is your personal research. In this day and age of technology and information overload, it's no rewarding to sit just to be fed. If you are hungry for facts and in search of answers for your curios mind then you must research in order to uncover the facts and truths that neither formal nor informal education will give you. You owe yourself a big deal to act now to seek knowledge. This will in turn yield wisdom for your personal revelation in relation to the one and only true *Most High* (the *Creator* of all the universe and everything in it visible and invisible to our naked eye).

The Bible has stated that giants (Nephilim) existed in the past prior to the flood and even some shorter giants after the flood. Let's look at **Genesis 6:4** *"There were giants in the earth in those days...."*. Archaeologists have dug out some of these giants which of course have been classified by the authorities in power. Most of these findings are hidden from the general public. However, you can research and easily come across some of these findings discovered by archaeologists and geographers.

Geographically and archaeologically, there are thousands of books out there that connect the disconnects in our world. With respect to the proof of the happenings of events in the bible to our material world which happens to be in uniformity with diverse records by the *Sumerian tablets*, *Qurʾān*, world cultures, histories and traditions. In my holistic perspective, a biblical and archaeological comparison was neatly done by Dr. H.L. Willmington in his book *Willmington's GUIDE to the BIBLE*. Check out page 948 to 968 where he categorically and precisely brought to light some of the findings and writings of archaeologists in support of the biblical stories and histories. He conveyed it right from the genesis era of creation through to the flood to the rise of mankind and all the kings, rulers, temples and other rich archaeological and biblical revelations depicting solid proofs of the biblical accounts of how humanity and our universe (earth) serve as a goldmine for what we have been searching for all our

lives.

THE ROLE OF SCIENCE and TECHOLOGY IN THE LOGIC OF GOD'S EXISTENCE.

God is the *"Supreme Energy"*. Science directly or indirectly contributes to the necessity in researching, learning, and walking the path of enlightenment to gravitate towards what our true core *(spirit)* yearns for every day. *The Most High* can take the shape of anything and everything *He* chooses. All branches of science have undisputable epistemological explanation of *energy*. Science is simply built on the *concepts of energy*. So, in retrospect, science is basically attempting to understand *The Most High (the Supreme being)*. Electromagnetic energy propagating through deep and shallow space in the form of x-rays, radio waves, ultraviolet, infrared, gamma rays and light are all part of *The Most High's* extensions of *Himself*. Every form of energy within and outside the form of *potential energy* and *kinetic energy* is part and parcel of

151

The Most High's omnipotence. The most powerful laws of physics are nothing but a thread of dust in the realm of *The Most High*. When the *spirit* separates from our earthly body, it results in going back to *The Most High*. By the way *The Most High* has many characteristics and that constitute an *energy*.

In all simplicity, science is basically a human approach to understanding the *being* and *nature* of *The Most High*. Epistemologically, it is very unscientific for my fellow science colleagues as well as some of the world-renowned scientists to loosely state that the universe just sprang into existence with no scientific proof or explanation as to *"what"* or *"who"* caused the initialization. Despite all the theories and complex formula known to mankind, the scientific world still falls short to proving how our world came into being without acknowledging an intelligent *Creator* known as *The Most High*. You cannot attempt to use material things from this physical world to see things within the spiritual realm. In that, the *energy* levels are different between both realms. All the greats in the scientific sector that have passed are encountering a different kind of reality in the spiritual realm. A reality that is separate from our physical realm whereby they cannot come back with all the scientific knowledge, theories and studies they left behind.

Science, just like any other branch of studies is an "acquired knowledge" managed and proposed by fellow human. So, the other question we fail to ask is, can the history, knowledge and workings of science be controlled by the nation/ethnic group in power? Who was the first human that started science? It definitely did not start in Europe, Asia or North America. In that, life did not begin from these parts of geographical locations. Life rather began in Africa, originally called *Mesopotamia.* The current Middle East is and has been part of Africa. It was just re-characterized and re-named as Middle East due to a controlled agenda by the nation that took/gained *"world power"* and influence. One can find this information with a simple scientific research online or library books, as a matter of fact just *"Google"* it. Information is everywhere, you can attain them if only you are willing to execute a little research. I state again that, you have not learned actual science if you do not know the basic history of science in the first place. If what comes to your mind with respect to science's first greats are European or North American scientists, then you need to do a little research because that is simply false and unscientific. Read about the University of Timbuktu in West Africa, known as the first ever university in the whole world obviously after Noah's flood.

All branches of science and academia known to mankind as well as the ones hidden from mankind started in Africa. I have great respect and admiration for science but there is an application that most people fail to use regardless of its common accessibility to mankind. That is the application of what I call, *philosophy of common sense*.

The *philosophy of common sense* is needed in all walks of

life. The word *"God"* is the English name for the *Creator*,

as I stated in chapter 3 on *"The Consciousness of God in*

Everything" that every nation, culture, ethnicity and

language has a name for *The Most High Creator*. I want to

emphasize again that, *The Most High* is everything. *He* is

the *"grand energy"*, the source of it all.

"Who" taught the *"first person"* in the universe about

science (Physical Sciences, Earth Sciences, Life Sciences)

in Astronomy, Oceanography, Mathematics, Physics,

Technology, Biology, Genetic Engineering and et al?

Where can you find this answer within all branches of

science epistemologically known to mankind? Science is

handicapped when *wisdom* is applied to go beyond what we

think we know and what we think we can prove. Science is

like a toddler, messing and playing around with his toys

thinking that the toys are the real thing. I have stated earlier that, I admire science and in no way do I intend to deny its usefulness, but science is not the answer to everything within our universe. Science as "human knowledge" can never crack the code of *The Most High*.

The *Annunaki* are known to the carnal man as the teachers of advanced science, spells and technologies *(the Sumerian texts unveil this aspect about the Annunaki)*. The *Book of Enoch* reveals who the *Annunaki* are. Knowing this fact will unfold to us *"who"* taught the *Annunaki* what they knew in order to teach people on planet earth about their attained knowledge.

Science is directly related to the *consciousness* or *soul* and not the *spirit*. In that science must *see*, *hold*, and *feel* the results before it believes that it is there. We all used to believe that there were nine planets in our solar system at one point. However, we were able to develop high technologies better than previous ones to detect galaxies far beyond what we knew back then. Now, we all accept the fact that, our universe doesn't have nine planets. Think about this, in the realms of galaxies upon galaxies; what does *"far"* mean? In that realm, the word or ideology of far is as relative as time is to us in the physical realm. Science can never in quadrillion years deny the existence of *The Most High Creator*. I can confidently predict that; science will eventually embrace *The Most High's* nature through its numerous discoveries. I just hope that it wouldn't be too late for many in the field of science who deny *The Most High Creator*.

If you believe in science and fail to believe in *The Most High*, then you are simply unwise because you are limited to the controlled knowledge of science. Which is simply a doctrine with limited knowledge to the true functioning of this universe. If you believe in science and also believe in *The Most High Creator*, then you are wise because science will propel you closer to your creator, *The Most High*.

This is about logic, epistemological reasoning and questioning to unleash your true self *(your spirit)* which is contained in the cage (our body). Most people within mankind are blind because they use the "dummy eyes" to see instead of their "true eye" which is not physical but spiritual. Science is necessary for mankind to survive on this planet but useless beyond this physical world upon death *(when we all transform to our true self a.k.a "spirit")*.

All science greats die, philosophy's greatest minds die, every human eventually will die. Science can never stop it. This has been attempted in the past before (pre-flood and pos-flood era). It didn't work, we are just using science to re-learn what happened in the past. We are not creating anything new.

Some few examples of science and technology trying to play god:

❖ Neural lace: upload or download any information into the human brain. It has been tested on mice.

❖ Genetically Modified Organisms whereby genes from DNAs of other organisms or plants are cross bred with a different kind or type of plant or organisms.

❖ Virtual and Filters are not *"real world"* reality: Using photoshops to appear different, something that you are not is gradually gravitating us to the age of virtual world. There is virtual romance, virtual family, virtual friends, virtual wife/fiancée/husband et al. Very soon, almost everyone would like to look like their filtered images (younger than their age, spotless-wrinkle free skin) and that is the fruition of virtual world. The world is heading there at a lightning speed.

Under technology, we are almost there in the machine and human flesh merged world. Another area technology is having a field day is hologram. Check out what holograms are currently being used to execute, science and technology is changing our world and everyday life pretty fast. Reality would be gone soon, and people would prefer filtered images (virtual images) over reality.

❖ What is the world going to use all the atomic and nuclear bombs for? Are we going to blow each other up or are we just going to use them as decorations? Yes, your rhetorical guess is on point. I am not frowning on technology; I am making a point that we as humans have lost our ways. Most of us are greedy, numb and heartless instead of love and compassion. Love and compassion will save the world, anything else is just doomed.

Wisdom is worth more than *knowledge, silver* and *gold*. **Hosea 4:6** is paraphrased as, people are *destroyed* for lack of <u>knowledge</u>. So, in rhetoric, if one is destroyed for lacking knowledge then what *happens to us* for *lack of* <u>wisdom</u>. Everything is cyclical, the nation (s) leading the world today would be leading from behind tomorrow. Historically, several civilizations rose to power for thousands of years and finally fell. It's part of the *energy* of life in our universe. Nothing last forever, per scientific researched data; our world will end eventually. The bible has also stated in the book of **Obadiah** *(KJV version)* that our world will end with all of its vain arrogant glory in space travel, interstellar travel, technology, wormhole studies and possible future explorations, discoveries of intergalactic waves within deep galaxies, black hole analysis and curious intent to explore, space occupancy, sophisticated inventions, et al will not save humanity. Humanity will self-destruct if we do not go back to the basics of love *(the core of our spirit)*. Only the faithful survive. In my perspective, all scientists are very knowledgeable, but a wise scientist is the one that uses the discoveries and theories of science to explain or gain a better comprehension about *The Most High*.

BIBLICAL RECORDS AND ACCOUNTS

Let me kick this section off by stating this fact that, the bible is not a religious book. *The Most High* has no religion. If you think of the bible as a religious movement then you are lost from the get-go. Let that sink in before we get started with our biblical discourse. Who created everything? Read the book of **Genesis *(Torah)*** gives an account of *The Most High* creating everything. <u>***What***</u> or <u>***who***</u> created the *Annunaki*? *The Most High* created everything, so *He* created the *Annunaki* also known as *"fallen angels"*. The *fallen angels* became the demons and evil spirits of this world who can no longer ascend to heaven. War happened in heaven whereby the dragon and his followers were cast down to earth. Earth became the dwelling place and ruling of these *fallen angels* or *Annunaki*.

Read *Genesis* chapter 6, for the sake of an emphasis; let's check out *Genesis 6:4-7 (KJV)* *"There were giants in the earth in those days; and also after that, when the sons of God came in unto the daughters of men, and they bare children to them, the same became mighty men which were of old, men of renown. ⁵ And God saw that the wickedness of man was great in the earth, and that every imagination of the thoughts of his heart was only evil continually. ⁶ And it repented the* LORD *that he had made man on the earth, and it grieved him at his heart. ⁷ And the* LORD *said, I will destroy man whom I have created from the face of the earth; both man, and beast, and the creeping thing, and the fowls of the air; for it repenteth me that I have made them"*.

Now, let's check out the ***Book of Enoch***, it is relevant for this point because *Enoch* wrote a comprehensive account about the *fallen angels/Annunaki*. *Enoch* wrote how they *(fallen angels/Annunaki)* taught mankind science, advanced technologies, how to read the stars, moon, spells, makeup (female cosmetics), et al. Who

was *Enoch*? Read **Genesis chapter 5** and **1st Chronicles 1**,

Enoch was the father of *Methuselah*, *Methuselah* had

Lamech, and *Lamech* had *Noah*.

The Book of Enoch Chapter 6:1 - 8
And it came to pass when the children of men had multiplied that in those days were born unto them beautiful and comely daughters. And the angels, the children of the heaven, saw and lusted after them, and said to one another: 'Come, let us choose us wives from among the children of men and beget us children.' And Semjaza, who was their leader, said unto them: 'I fear ye will not indeed agree to do this deed, and I alone shall have to pay the penalty of a great sin.' And they all answered him and said: 'Let us all swear an oath, and all bind ourselves by mutual imprecations not to abandon this plan but to do this thing.' Then sware they all together and bound themselves by mutual imprecations upon it. And they were in all two hundred; who descended in the days of Jared on the summit of Mount Hermon, and they called it Mount Hermon, because they had sworn and bound themselves by mutual imprecations upon it. And these are the names of their leaders: Samlazaz, their leader, Araklba, Rameel, Kokablel, Tamlel, Ramlel, Danel, Ezeqeel, Baraqijal, Asael, Armaros, Batarel, Ananel, Zaqiel, Samsapeel, Satarel, Turel, Jomjael, Sariel. These are their chiefs of tens.

The Book of Enoch Chapter 7:1 – 6

And all the others together with them took unto themselves wives, and each chose for himself one, and they began to go in unto them and to defile themselves with them, and they taught them charms and enchantments, and the cutting of roots, and made them acquainted with plants. And they became pregnant, and they bare great giants, whose height was three thousand ells: Who consumed all the acquisitions of men. And when men could no longer sustain them, the giants turned against them and devoured mankind. And they began to sin against birds, and beasts, and reptiles, and fish, and to devour one another's flesh, and drink the blood. Then the earth laid accusation against the lawless ones.

The Book of Enoch Chapter 8:1 – 3

And Azazel taught men to make swords, and knives, and shields, and breastplates, and made known to them the metals of the earth and the art of working them, and bracelets, and ornaments, and the use of antimony, and the beautifying of the eyelids, and all kinds of costly stones, and all colouring tinctures. And there arose much godlessness, and they committed fornication, and they were led astray, and became corrupt in all their ways. Semjaza taught enchantments, and root-cuttings, 'Armaros the resolving of enchantments, Baraqijal (taught) astrology, Kokabel the constellations, Ezeqeel the knowledge of the clouds, Araqiel the signs of the earth, Shamsiel the signs of the sun, and Sariel the course of the moon. And as men perished, they cried, and their cry went up to heaven.

Continue to read, *The Book of Enoch Chapter 9:1 – 10, Chapter 14, Chapter 15, Chapter 16, Chapter 17, Chapter 18, Chapter 20 and Chapter 21.* Think well about it and make sure to take notes.

Let's look at the following verses from the *KJV* bible about

the devil, main leader of the *fallen angels (one third of the*

angels in heaven fell to become demons):

Isiah 14:12 – 17
[12] *How art thou fallen from heaven, O Lucifer, son of the morning! how art thou cut down to the ground, which didst weaken the nations!*

[13] *For thou hast said in thine heart, I will ascend into heaven, I will exalt my throne above the stars of God: I will sit also upon the mount of the congregation, in the sides of the north:*

[14] *I will ascend above the heights of the clouds; I will be like the most High.*

[15] *Yet thou shalt be brought down to hell, to the sides of the pit.*

[16] *They that see thee shall narrowly look upon thee, and consider thee, saying, Is this the man that made the earth to tremble, that did shake kingdoms;*

[17] *That made the world as a wilderness, and destroyed the cities thereof; that opened not the house of his prisoners?*

There are more bible verses about the devil and the

fallen angels including the following: Ezekiel 28:12 – 19

(Old Testament book) and the Christians view in their *New*

Testament books of Revelation 12: 7 – 9, John 12:31, II

Corinthians 4:4, 1 John 5:19, and Revelation 20:10.

Old Testament's Biblical Record on The Birth of Two Nations. The Torah's Record.

The world's population can easily be summed up into two nations with one underlining source of biological origination. Currently, the world's population is approaching 8 billion. It is very easy for anyone to doubt that mankind is connected to only one source of family. However, both the bible and scientific dna make it possible for us to identify this truth. The book of *Genesis 25:19-26* introduces us to the two nations, *v.23-26* records that; the first born was <u>red</u> all over and <u>hairy</u>, his name was *Esau*. *Jacob (the twin brother)* then came out of his mother's womb. This was the first introduction of the *"red nation"*. Entire genealogies (from Adam to Isaac and Ishmael) prior to *Genesis 25* had no mention of a *"red" person "thread-like" garment hair all over the body.*

Alternatively, they were all like *Jacob's <u>tone</u>* including *Jacob's* parents. This is why *Jacob's* appearance was not emphasized when he was born. I need to put out the disclosure that, this is not about race; it has everything to do with our ability to go back to where mankind originated from and how our diverse backgrounds, cultures, mentality and aspirations were influenced. *Jacob (a dark melanated man)* is the nation of *Israel (12 tribes of Israel represents the 12 sons of Jacob)*. *Isaac*, father of the twins *(Esau and Jacob)* is the promised son of *Abraham*. *The Most High Creator* had a covenant with *Abraham*, read about this in **Genesis 17**. *Jacob's* posterity, *King Solomon (King David's* son) emphasized his *blackness* or *dark melanin* in **Song of Solomon 1:5,6.**

Esau is the *"red nation"* or *Edom/Edomites*, they lived around the *caucasus mountains* which was originally known as *Mount Seir* as stated in **Genesis 36:8.** Edom/Edomites intermingled and intermarried with the progenies of *Ishmael* (*Abraham's* son with *Hagar*, the concubine/handmaid), posterity of *Keturah's* six sons (*Keturah* was also a concubine of *Abraham*, **Genesis 25: 1-6 and 1ˢᵗ Chronicles 1:32,33**). The intermarrying of *"red nation"* and other groups stated above including some granddaughters and great granddaughters and sons of *Noah* (through his sons' offsprings that sailed to settle as far as *Asia*, *Europe* and other parts of the world including *Africa*).

Keturah's children also assimilated with *Ishmael's* posterity. It is factually safe to say that the Islamic religion sprang from *Ishmael's* line with some of *Keturah's* children. *Edomites* had pride and anger towards *Jacob* and *The Most High*. The nation of *Edom* went into idol/image worshipping and other various pagan practices like that of *Nimrod (i.e. the King of Babylon who built the tower of Babel, one of Noah's grandsons, whose father was Cush, son of Ham recorded in* **Genesis 10:10, Genesis 11***).* Pagan worship with the influence of *Nimrod* worshipped on

Sunday, sun worshippers. They worshipped *Nimrod* as a "sun god" instead of worshipping on the sabbath, a day ordained by *The Most High*. A brief synopsis about the genesis of this pagan worship comes in light with *Semiramis'* fabrication of a story that *Nimrod* returned to her from the sun in the form of a sun ray to impregnate her after *Nimrod's* death. The baby born was named *Tammuz* (the *pagan's trinity* was then initiated, orchestrated by the devil as it involves human sacrifice). The *sun god* worship then spread out into many nations and generations throughout history to this day.

The *fallen angels or Annunaki* were full of knowledge because they were in the presence of the Omniscient, *All Knowing Most High Creator* prior to their fall. The *fallen angels'* knowledge is powerful beyond human's comprehension. They have been in dissimulation to create duplications of the knowledge, teachings, and creations of *The Most High Creator* to deceive humans.

171

These *fallen angels/Annunaki* are good at creating synthetic realities by mimicking *The Most High*. For an individual to be able to detect the synthetic realities created by these *fallen angels/Annunaki*; one has to be *spiritual*. You can never use your carnal mind to understand spiritual things. Most of the churches today are worshiping the *sun god* and not *The Most High Creator* of the universe.

Caucasians (etymology of the "caucasus mountains" also known as *Mount Seir*) are the *Edomites/Idumeans (Idumea)/Esau's* descendants, read **Genesis 36** below:

1Now these are the generations of Esau, who is Edom.

2 Esau took his wives of the daughters of Canaan; Adah the daughter of Elon the Hittite, and Aholibamah the daughter of Anah the daughter of Zibeon the Hivite;

3 And Bashemath Ishmael's daughter, sister of Nebajoth.

4 And Adah bare to Esau Eliphaz; and Bashemath bare Reuel;

5 And Aholibamah bare Jeush, and Jaalam, and Korah: these are the sons of Esau, which were born unto him in the land of Canaan.

6 And Esau took his wives, and his sons, and his daughters, and all the persons of his house, and his cattle, and all his beasts, and all his substance, which he had got in the land of Canaan; and went into the country from the face of his brother Jacob.

7 For their riches were more than that they might dwell together; and the land wherein they were strangers could not bear them because of their cattle.

8 Thus dwelt Esau in mount Seir: Esau is Edom.

9 And these are the generations of Esau the father of the Edomites in mount Seir:

10 These are the names of Esau's sons; Eliphaz the son of Adah the wife of Esau, Reuel the son of Bashemath the wife of Esau.

11 And the sons of Eliphaz were Teman, Omar, Zepho, and Gatam, and Kenaz.

12 And Timna was concubine to Eliphaz Esau's son; and she bare to Eliphaz Amalek: these were the sons of Adah Esau's wife.

13 And these are the sons of Reuel; Nahath, and Zerah, Shammah, and Mizzah: these were the sons of Bashemath Esau's wife.

14 And these were the sons of Aholibamah, the daughter of Anah the daughter of Zibeon, Esau's wife: and she bare to Esau Jeush, and Jaalam, and Korah.

15 These were dukes of the sons of Esau: the sons of Eliphaz the firstborn son of Esau; duke Teman, duke Omar, duke Zepho, duke Kenaz,

16 Duke Korah, duke Gatam, and duke Amalek: these are the dukes that came of Eliphaz in the land of Edom; these were the sons of Adah.

17 And these are the sons of Reuel Esau's son; duke Nahath, duke Zerah, duke Shammah, duke Mizzah: these are the dukes that came of Reuel in the land of Edom; these are the sons of Bashemath Esau's wife.

18 And these are the sons of Aholibamah Esau's wife; duke Jeush, duke Jaalam, duke Korah: these were the dukes that came of Aholibamah the daughter of Anah, Esau's wife.

19 These are the sons of Esau, who is Edom, and these are their dukes.

20 These are the sons of Seir the Horite, who inhabited the land; Lotan, and Shobal, and Zibeon, and Anah,

21 And Dishon, and Ezer, and Dishan: these are the dukes of the Horites, the children of Seir in the land of Edom.

22 And the children of Lotan were Hori and Hemam; and Lotan's sister was Timna.

23 And the children of Shobal were these; Alvan, and Manahath, and Ebal, Shepho, and Onam.

24 And these are the children of Zibeon; both Ajah, and Anah: this was that Anah that found the mules in the wilderness, as he fed the asses of Zibeon his father.

25 And the children of Anah were these; Dishon, and Aholibamah the daughter of Anah.

26 And these are the children of Dishon; Hemdan, and Eshban, and Ithran, and Cheran.

27 The children of Ezer are these; Bilhan, and Zaavan, and Akan.

28 The children of Dishan are these; Uz, and Aran.

29 These are the dukes that came of the Horites; duke Lotan, duke Shobal, duke Zibeon, duke Anah,

30 Duke Dishon, duke Ezer, duke Dishan: these are the dukes that came of Hori, among their dukes in the land of Seir.

31 And these are the kings that reigned in the land of Edom, before there reigned any king over the children of Israel.

32 And Bela the son of Beor reigned in Edom: and the name of his city was Dinhabah.

33 And Bela died, and Jobab the son of Zerah of Bozrah reigned in his stead.

34 And Jobab died, and Husham of the land of Temani reigned in his stead.

35 And Husham died, and Hadad the son of Bedad, who smote Midian in the field of Moab, reigned in his stead: and the name of his city was Avith.

36 And Hadad died, and Samlah of Masrekah reigned in his stead.

37 And Samlah died, and Saul of Rehoboth by the river reigned in his stead.

38 And Saul died, and Baalhanan the son of Achbor reigned in his stead.

39 And Baalhanan the son of Achbor died, and Hadar reigned in his stead: and the name of his city was Pau; and his wife's name was Mehetabel, the daughter of Matred, the daughter of Mezahab.

40 And these are the names of the dukes that came of Esau, according to their families, after their places, by their names; duke Timnah, duke Alvah, duke Jetheth,

41 Duke Aholibamah, duke Elah, duke Pinon,

42 Duke Kenaz, duke Teman, duke Mibzar,

43 Duke Magdiel, duke Iram: these be the dukes of Edom, according to their habitations in the land of their possession: he is Esau the father of the Edomites.

A more condensed version of *Edomites* or *Idumeans*

a.k.a *Caucasians/Esau* is found at **1 Chronicles 1:35-54**.

35 The sons of Esau; Eliphaz, Reuel, and Jeush, and Jaalam, and

Korah.

36 The sons of Eliphaz; Teman, and Omar, Zephi, and Gatam, Kenaz,

and Timna, and Amalek.

37 The sons of Reuel; Nahath, Zerah, Shammah, and Mizzah.

[38] *And the sons of Seir; Lotan, and Shobal, and Zibeon, and Anah, and Dishon, and Ezar, and Dishan.*

[39] *And the sons of Lotan; Hori, and Homam: and Timna was Lotan's sister.*

[40] *The sons of Shobal; Alian, and Manahath, and Ebal, Shephi, and Onam. and the sons of Zibeon; Aiah, and Anah.*

[41] *The sons of Anah; Dishon. And the sons of Dishon; Amram, and Eshban, and Ithran, and Cheran.*

[42] *The sons of Ezer; Bilhan, and Zavan, and Jakan. The sons of Dishan; Uz, and Aran.*

[43] *Now these are the kings that reigned in the land of Edom before any king reigned over the children of Israel; Bela the son of Beor: and the name of his city was Dinhabah.*

[44] *And when Bela was dead, Jobab the son of Zerah of Bozrah reigned in his stead.*

[45] *And when Jobab was dead, Husham of the land of the Temanites reigned in his stead.*

[46] *And when Husham was dead, Hadad the son of Bedad, which smote Midian in the field of Moab, reigned in his stead: and the name of his city was Avith.*

[47] *And when Hadad was dead, Samlah of Masrekah reigned in his stead.*

[48] *And when Samlah was dead, Shaul of Rehoboth by the river reigned in his stead.*

[49] *And when Shaul was dead, Baalhanan the son of Achbor reigned in his stead.*

[50] And when Baalhanan was dead, Hadad reigned in his stead: and the name of his city was Pai; and his wife's name was Mehetabel, the daughter of Matred, the daughter of Mezahab.

[51] Hadad died also. And the dukes of Edom were; duke Timnah, duke Aliah, duke Jetheth,

[52] Duke Aholibamah, duke Elah, duke Pinon,

[53] Duke Kenaz, duke Teman, duke Mibzar,

[54] Duke Magdiel, duke Iram. These are the dukes of Edom.

It appears that *Caucasians* still use title like *"Duke"* from their old ancestors. The entire European continent throughout Middle East (Old North Africa) also known as the Arabian peninsula are all classified as *Caucasians* per academia, history and dictionary definitions. Let's dive into the Roman Empire that was constituted by the Byzantine Kingdom (Eastern Empire) and the Western Kingdom (Western Empire) to find out what countries were made up of this Roman empire. What we call the *"western world"* in today's term is simply the Western Empire/Kingdom of the old Roman empire. The Byzantine empire collapsed, and later became the Middle

East as most of us know of today. As usual, I encourage

you to research into how the Middle East was formed by

the Great Britain and United States. Pay attention to the

details and its biblical implications that caused the original

Israelites *(Jacob's descendants a.k.a the 12 tribes of Israel)*

to lose their nationality as Israelites. This sparked the

Trans-Atlantic slave trade; first by the *Caucasian Arabs*

and then later by the Europeans and the United States. Read

Psalm 83:1-8 below to see how *Caucasians* a.k.a

Edomites/Idumeans joined forces with other

Ishmaelites/Arabs to destroy the identity of the Israelites

(dark melanin twelve tribes/children of *Jacob*) as a nation.

*1Keep not thou silence, O God: hold not thy peace, and be not still, O
God.*

*[2] For, lo, thine enemies make a tumult: and they that hate thee have
lifted up the head.*
*[3] **They have taken crafty counsel against thy people, and consulted
against thy hidden ones.***
*[4] **They have said, Come, and <u>let us cut them off from being a nation;</u>
that the name of Israel may be no more in remembrance.***

⁵ For they have consulted together with one consent: they are confederate against thee:

⁶ The tabernacles of Edom, and the Ishmaelites; of Moab, and the Hagarenes;

⁷ Gebal, and Ammon, and Amalek; the Philistines with the inhabitants of Tyre;

⁸ Assur also is joined with them: they have holpen the children of Lot. Selah.

The Trans-Atlantic slave trade in ***Deuteronomy 28:68*** (read the entire chapter to fully comprehend) indicates that:

68 And the LORD shall bring thee into Egypt <u>again</u> with <u>ships,</u> by the way whereof I spake unto thee, Thou shalt see it no more again: and there <u>ye shall be sold unto your enemies</u> for bondmen and bondwomen, and <u>no man shall buy you</u>.

The true descendants of *Jacob* or the 12 tribes of Israel are mostly heavily melanated scattered throughout *Africa (Ghana, Nigeria, Ethiopia, South Africa and other African countries).* Some were taken through the Trans-Atlantic slave trade to the Americas and all over the world. The current *Caucasians/Edomites* occupying the land of

Israel are converts from *Gomer* a descendant of *Japhet*.

These are not the biological or bloodline of *Jacob (The*

Chosen one) who is under *Shem*. Research further for an

exciting revelation of our world in relation to the topic of

discussion.

There are more than one hundred books that

Edomites/Caucasian Roman Catholics influenced through

the Council of Nicaea to remove from the bible. The

Edomite's classified those books as *"apocryphal"* but I

highly encourage you to read them in order to know the full

history of the bible. These books that was "supposedly"

rejected by *Edomites/Caucasians* reveal more secrets about

them and aid you to easily track most of the atrocities they

did do the original Israelites. In the book of ***Jasher 90:7-9;***

it exposes how the *Edomites* became one kingdom

under/with *"Chittim"* known as Rome (*Japhet's*

descendants in ***Genesis 10:1-5***). Read more in ***Amos 1***; this

is actual history as well as prophetic tied to **Obadiah 1.**

To my science fanatics who may have some questions on a biological level with respect to dna validation while reading these biblical accounts; I will say that, deoxyribonucleic acid testing (dna testing) under the auspices of science solidifies the biological linkage of mankind to one source (family). Scientifically, every human being constitutes some percentage of the *dark melanated nation's* dna (due to ancestral linkage of mankind since the time of melanated *Adam*).

On the other hand, people mix with *"red"/Edomites'* dna possesses the traits of the red nation's dna. If you happened to be one of the few that fracas to believe what the bible says in regard to mankind's biological oneness; then use science (dna testing) to help you comprehend, discover and reverence the power and audacity of *The Most High*. People with rapacious propensities came up with the fallacious race propaganda which has destroyed the very fabric of human's unity in diversity.

One thing worth noting on this topic is the *book of **Obadiah***. According to this book, there is a judgement set for *Edomites/Idumeans/Esau's* descendants. This is what the book of ***Obadiah*** says:

1The vision of Obadiah. Thus saith the Lord GOD concerning Edom; We have heard a rumour from the LORD, and an ambassador is sent among the heathen, Arise ye, and let us rise up against her in battle.
² Behold, I have made thee small among the heathen: thou art greatly despised.
³ The pride of thine heart hath deceived thee, thou that dwellest in the clefts of the rock, whose habitation is high; that saith in his heart, Who shall bring me down to the ground?
⁴ Though thou exalt thyself as the eagle, and though thou set thy nest among the stars, thence will I bring thee down, saith the LORD.
⁵ If thieves came to thee, if robbers by night, (how art thou cut off!) would they not have stolen till they had enough? if the grapegatherers came to thee, would they not leave some grapes?
⁶ How are the things of Esau searched out! how are his hidden things sought up!
⁷ All the men of thy confederacy have brought thee even to the border: the men that were at peace with thee have deceived thee, and prevailed

against thee; they that eat thy bread have laid a wound under thee: there is none understanding in him.

[8] Shall I not in that day, saith the LORD, even destroy the wise men out of Edom, and understanding out of the mount of Esau?

[9] And thy mighty men, O Teman, shall be dismayed, to the end that every one of the mount of Esau may be cut off by slaughter.

[10] For thy violence against thy brother Jacob shame shall cover thee, and thou shalt be cut off for ever.

[11] In the day that thou stoodest on the other side, in the day that the strangers carried away captive his forces, and foreigners entered into his gates, and cast lots upon Jerusalem, even thou wast as one of them.

[12] But thou shouldest not have looked on the day of thy brother in the day that he became a stranger; neither shouldest thou have rejoiced over the children of Judah in the day of their destruction; neither shouldest thou have spoken proudly in the day of distress.

[13] Thou shouldest not have entered into the gate of my people in the day of their calamity; yea, thou shouldest not have looked on their affliction in the day of their calamity, nor have laid hands on their substance in the day of their calamity;

[14] Neither shouldest thou have stood in the crossway, to cut off those of his that did escape; neither shouldest thou have delivered up those of his that did remain in the day of distress.

[15] For the day of the LORD is near upon all the heathen: as thou hast done, it shall be done unto thee: thy reward shall return upon thine own head.

[16] For as ye have drunk upon my holy mountain, so shall all the heathen drink continually, yea, they shall drink, and they shall swallow down, and they shall be as though they had not been.

[17] *But upon mount Zion shall be deliverance, and there shall be holiness; and the house of Jacob shall possess their possessions.*
[18] *And the house of Jacob shall be a fire, and the house of Joseph a flame, and the house of Esau for stubble, and they shall kindle in them, and devour them; and there shall not be any remaining of the house of Esau; for the LORD hath spoken it.*
[19] *And they of the south shall possess the mount of Esau; and they of the plain the Philistines: and they shall possess the fields of Ephraim, and the fields of Samaria: and Benjamin shall possess Gilead.*
[20] *And the captivity of this host of the children of Israel shall possess that of the Canaanites, even unto Zarephath; and the captivity of Jerusalem, which is in Sepharad, shall possess the cities of the south.*
[21] *And saviours shall come up on mount Zion to judge the mount of Esau; and the kingdom shall be the LORD's.*

What you make of the *book of* **Obadiah** is dependent on your belief, doctrines and understanding of the bible. These are the words of *Prophet Obadiah* as directed by *The Most High*. Study it and research more into it to have a solid understanding of this powerful yet interesting book in the bible.

In *2 Esdras 6:9* it states that:

"For Esau is the end of the world, and Jacob is the beginning of it that followeth." This is also an indication that the 12 tribes of Israel, the original Israelites will eventually be in charge of everything after Esau or Edom/Idumea a.k.a Caucasians' time is over with.

JACOB'S LINEAGE

The bible is not just a book but also a collection of cultures, laws, and traditions of heavily melanated people known as the *Ebrew Israelites* (the term known to modern society is *"Hebrew"*). The word *"Hebrew"* is a corruption of its original word *"Ebers"* which means descendants of *Eber*, son of *Shem*. Most of *Eber's* lineage followed the laws and commandments of *The Most High*.

Fig.33

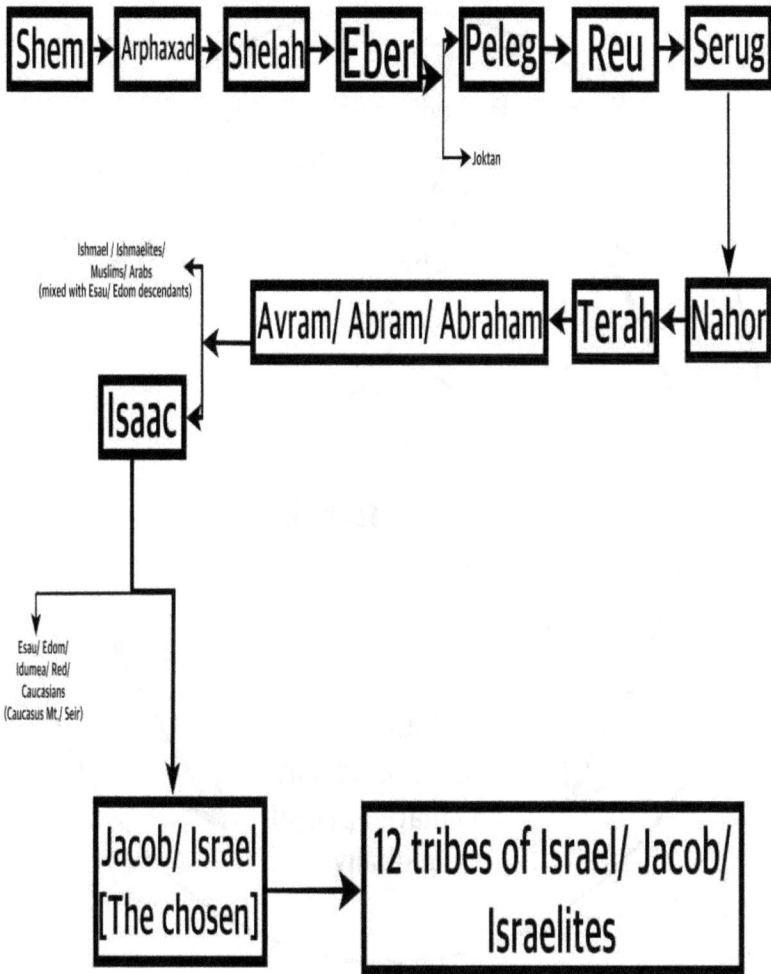

Fig.34

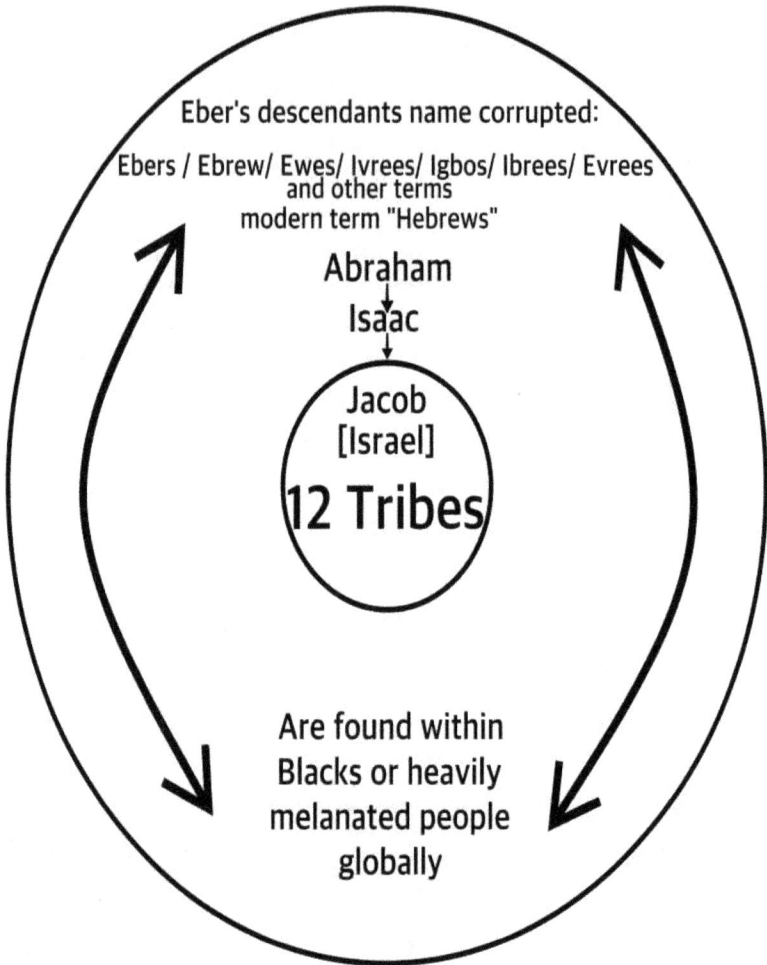

Eber's descendants name corrupted:
Ebers / Ebrew/ Ewes/ Ivrees/ Igbos/ Ibrees/ Evrees
and other terms
modern term "Hebrews"

Abraham
↓
Isaac
↓

Jacob
[Israel]
12 Tribes

Are found within
Blacks or heavily
melanated people
globally

Note: All *Ebrews/Hebrews* are **not** Israelites, but all Israelites are *Ebrews/Hebrews*. These Israelites are currently not living on the physical land called Israel. The twelve tribes of Jacob/Israel have been dispersed throughout the four corners of the earth with majority of them currently living in Africa. The western part of Africa is known to have a lot of these Israelites. The trans-atlantic slave trade captured most of the Israelites from the tribe of Judah into the Americas, other parts of Europe and the rest of the African diaspora. You can read **Deuteronomy 28:66-68** to learn about the trans-atlantic slave trade and **Psalm 83** as discussed previously about how the nationality and identity of *Israel* was taken and destroyed by the *Edomites/Idumeans/Esau* together with *Ishmaelites* and *Japhet*. Lastly, groups like the Banktu, Akans, Ga-Adangbe and many other ethnicities or tribes under the lineage of *Eber* (Look at the genealogy of Shem in **Genesis 10:22-32**) to get the entire picture.

I encourage you to research who *Edom/Idumea* is just in case you don't know. Look into *1525 Jewish Encyclopedia, Vol. 5*; *Jewish Almanac 1980; Encyclopedia Judaica 1971 Vol. 10:23*. As you may be very much aware now, I have been encouraging you through what I call *the philosophy of research and knowledge seeking* to execute research of your own because that is a tool for your spiritual, intellectual and social emancipation.

The Most High Yahuah Maccadddeshoem is *Sabbaoth* and definitely shouldn't be mocked like how the fictional *New Testament* paints *Him*. We should all be careful with our attempts to scorn *The Most High* because we are a people full of insincerity, immorality, and are definitely indebted. We do not own our lives, it was given to us. We all die. Hence, the providence is only of *The Most High. The Most High* is the *Adonai, Roi, El, Elyon, Elohim, Shalom, Jireh, Nissi, Shammah, Rapha* and definitely cannot be scorned or cheated. The Most High loved *Jacob* (melanated "original blood line" of the 12 tribes of Israel); let's look at **Genesis 28:3-4; 28:13-15; 35:11-12; 1 Chronicles 16:17; Deuteronomy 1:8; 4:37; 7:8; 13; 10:15; 15:16; 23:5; 33:3; Isaiah 43:4; 48:14; 63:9; Jeremiah 5:20; 10:16; 30:18; 31:3; Hosea 3:1; 11:1 and 4; 14:4; Malachi 1:2-3; Exodus 3:6; Amos 9:8.**

The entire nation of *Edom* or *Idumea* was very wicked and continue to be a wicked nation. This wicked nation is a bloodline decendants of *Esau,* who *The Most High* hates and has set *His* judgement against them to *"cut off"* their existence per **Obadiah 1:10** *"For thy violence against thy brother Jacob shame shall cover thee, and thou shalt be CUT OFF*

FOR EVER." *Idumeans* or *Edomites* assisted and joined the

Ishmaelites (Arabians) and *Philistines* during their

destruction of Jerusalem, ***2Chron. 21:16, 17; Obadiah 11,***

12, 13, 14. Let's look at *Edom/Idumea* a.k.a *Esau* with the

following illustrations reflecting what the nation of

Idumea/Edom has been up to throughout history.

Fig.35

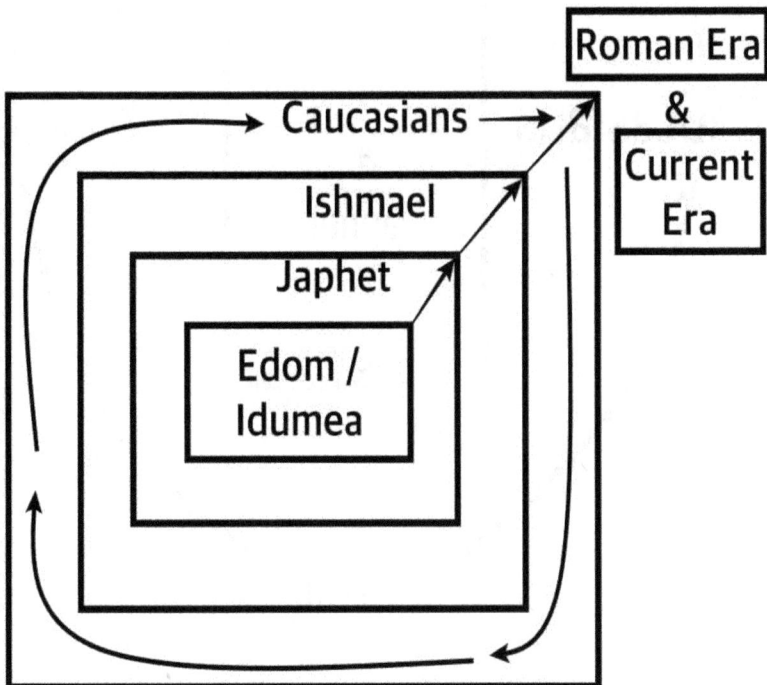

Fig.36

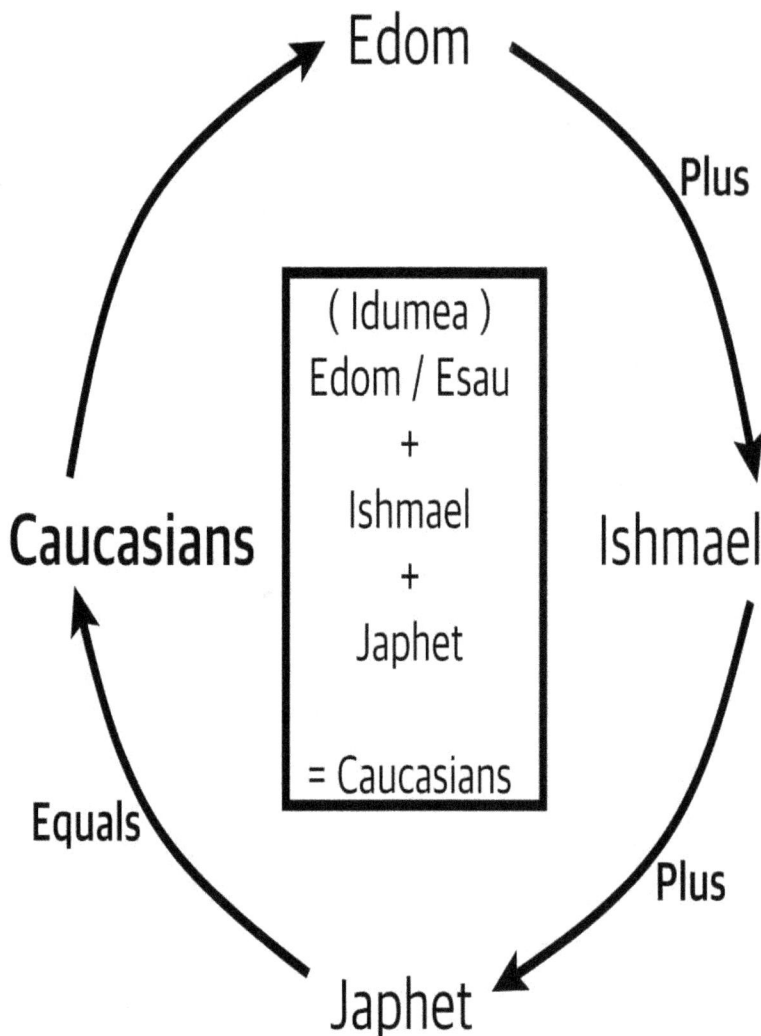

NOTE: Edom/Idumea/Esau also impregnated some of the daughters of Ham. Esau or Edom was adulterous per Torah.

Fig.37   Edomites, Ishmael and Japhet joined together.

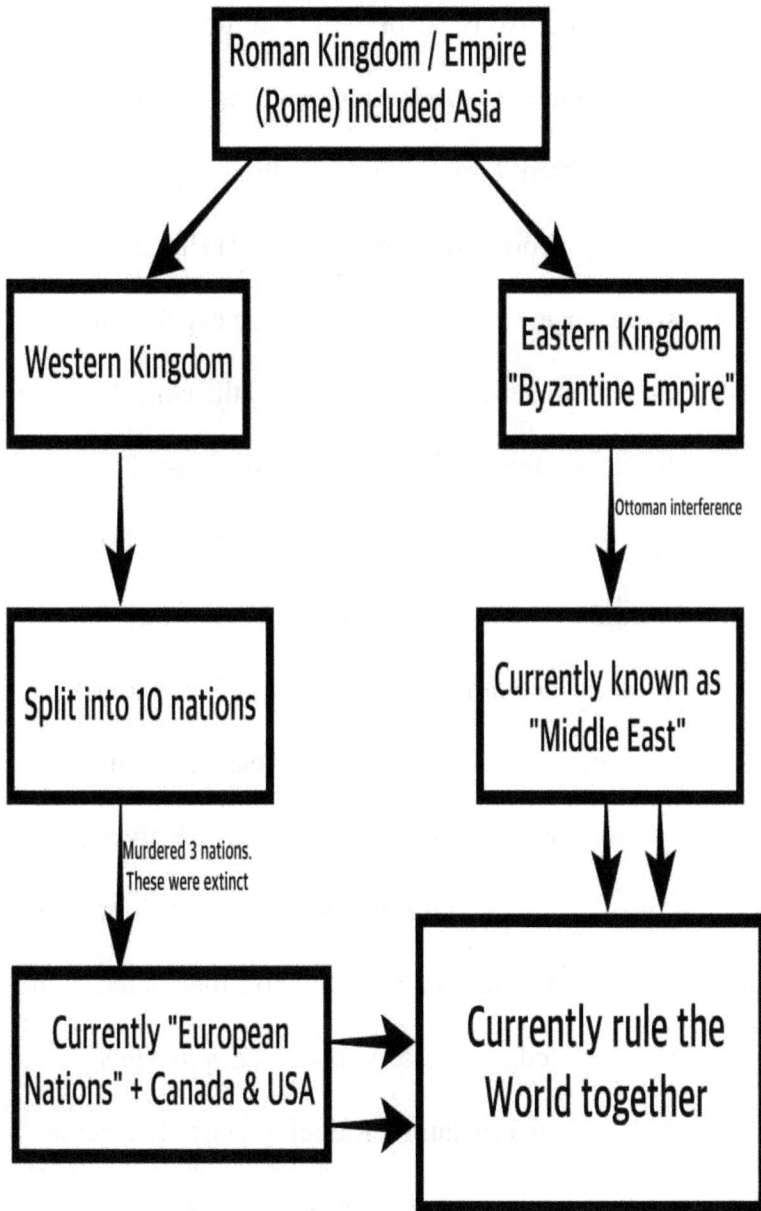

CONCLUDING STATEMENT FOR THIS JOURNEY

There are two types of people in the world, there are those with melanin production and those without melanin production. Melanin protects the body from sun damages; think about how ultraviolet (UV) shield is used in sunglasses. Hence, melanin protects those capable of producing it from severe sun damages to the skin. Melanin is also the reason for the "color" of the skin just like chlorophyll in plants enables the plants to absorb light energy from the sun or any source of light during photosynthesis. The other group of people who cannot produce melanin need sunscreen as a means of skin protectant from the sun. We see that the *Torah* gives an account of such *"gene mutation"* (scientific word/term) by *The Most High* in **Genesis 25:25**; the non-melanated twin of *Jacob* was called *Esau* also known as *Edom/Idumea*. *Esau* didn't have the melanin producing gene. The verse also states that *Esau* was *"hairy **all over** like a garment"*;

meaning long thread-like hair and full body hair. According to the knowledge in genetic science, a recessive gene disorder causes the non-melanin production in humans. It is also obvious that we all came from one family, but we do not look identical. Have a look at your biological twin or sibling, do you look one hundred percent identical? Obviously not. Race and color classifications are false, a sham, scientifically unprovable and a huge fallacy.

I have motivated you throughout this book to research, seek more knowledge and most importantly wisdom and direction from *The Most High* because ignorance of these truths only put you at a psychological and spiritual disadvantage.

From the *Torah* accounts and perspective of creation, it also appears that everything comes in pairs. In the form of life and death, spiritual and physical, positive and negative flow of energy, day and night, north and south, east and west, up and down, right and left, man and woman, physical death and spiritual death, physical life and spiritual life, physical realm and spiritual realm, a pair of eyes, ears, hands, brain divided into two, heart, legs, lips, even animals come in pairs, et al. There are spiritual powers/influences working and flowing through, in and around us undetected by our physical eyes. We have the *power* via *Free Will* to choose *"who"* or *"what"* to believe, accept, welcome and follow in our lives. At the end of the day, it all depends on you; whether your *spirit* (your true self) lives eternally in joy or suffers eternally.

Acquire as much knowledge as you can, live as large or as small as you can, be free, enjoy this brief yet precious moment in this physical realm. It's just a transitional preparation for the grand purpose. You are created for eternity no matter your choices in life but there is/are consequences or rewards. It is very common for the super-rich in this physical realm to be the poorest in the spiritual realm and the poorest in this physical realm to be the richest in the spiritual realm.

Do not fall prey to the seductive call of gullibility. You may not even taste it because it is tasteless. You may not feel it because it is numb to the soul (your consciousness). You may not see it because it is undetectable to the physical eyes, and you cannot hear it because it is inaudible. Only those who transcend spiritually understand the things of the spirit. Anyone who struggles with it is just carnal. The carnal individual is spiritually dead to the things of the spirit. If you ask me what *spirituality* is, I will simply define *spirituality* as the absolute *frequency* that *vibrates* your *energy*. Make sure you choose wisely on your spiritual journey because you have no one to blame but yourself.

REFERENCE

Willmington, H. L. (1981). *Willmingtons GUIDE to the BIBLE*. Carol Stream,, IL: Tyndale House.

(Mentioned in Chp.7 under Archaeology)

KJV Bible verses (public domain).

REFERENCE TO THE BOOK OF ENOCH

The Book of Enoch

Chapter 6:1-8

Chapter 7:1-6

Chapter 8:1-3

Chapter 9:1-10

Chapter 14

Chapter 15

Chapter 16

Chapter 17

Chapter 18

Chapter 20

Chapter 21

<u>NOTES</u>

NOTES

<u>NOTES</u>

<u>NOTES</u>

Thank you for Reading and Studying

GOD'S AUDACITY:
The Logic of GOD'S EXISTENCE

by

Samuel K. Anderson

ABOUT THE AUTHOR:

Samuel K. Anderson (BSBA, MBA, University of The Incarnate Word) is a Ghanaian American citizen and a member of the largest leadership honor society in the nation (United States of America) known as NSLS, The National Society of Leadership and Success. He has served as an astute leader, motivator, philanthropist, father, entrepreneur, mentor, wisdom seeker and educator.

He is a vibrant CEO and founder of two companies. A motivational and life coach speaker. He served in his early formal education years as the Regional Trustee for the Eastern Regional Students' Representative Council with the Council's aim to Emancipate Students through Dialogue and a Philosophy of Non-Violence, President of an NGO that aimed at educating the youths on drug abuse, Counsellor, Director of Children's Ministry, and Teacher to second grade students. He completed formal bible training education, enrolled at Seminary School for a while and also studied Theology at Central University College before transitioning to San Antonio College then transferred to University of The Incarnate Word to pursue bachelor's degree in Accounting and an MBA graduate level degree with concentration in Asset Management (Real Estate and Finance).

www.ingramcontent.com/pod-product-compliance
Lightning Source LLC
Chambersburg PA
CBHW051904090426
42811CB00003B/455